Dear Theo

letters to a friend

illustrated by

JASON RAMASAMI

Biblica provides God's Word to people through translation,
publishing and Bible engagement in Africa, Asia Pacific, Europe,
Latin America, Middle East, and North America. Through its
worldwide reach, Biblica engages people with God's Word so that
their lives are transformed through a relationship with Jesus Christ.

Dear Theo is part of our transformational Bible reading programme known as
Community Bible Experience. Find out more at www.biblicaeurope.com/cbe.

Eng. NT NIrV   9/17; Printed in UK

Contents

Note to reader v
Reading plan vi
5 Questions vii
Luke investigates viii
Meet the characters x
Where is this story going? xii
Introduction xv

Luke

One 1
Two 23
Three 59
Four 103

Acts

Five 135
Six 159
Seven 175
Eight 189
Nine 207
Ten 221

Living the story 260
Community Bible Experience 262

Note to reader

Dr Luke was so excited about the story of Jesus and his followers that he wanted to make sure his friend Theo had all the facts written down clearly.

We are also very excited about this story and wanted to present it in a way that makes it easy for you to read.

So, we took what Luke wrote right out of the Bible (where you usually find this story) and made it look more like the books you are used to reading. We took the words from a version of the Bible called the *New International Readers' Version* which was produced especially for people your age and added some pictures to help you understand the story even better.

Dear Theo can be read like any other book but really comes alive when you chat about what you're reading with others. A fun and easy way to do this is to meet once a week with friends or family who are also reading *Dear Theo*.

This could be at home, school or church. Why not ask your youth leader, teacher or parent to help set this up?

The following pages and our website have helpful information on ways to do this and questions that will help you as you explore the story together.

Dr Luke's life was changed so much by Jesus that he just had to pass on the news about him to others. We hope this new presentation of his story helps you read it, talk about it and pass it on to your friends as well.

Reading plan

The reading plan below provides a helpful structure for using *Dear Theo* in different settings – home, church, school, etc. You could read for 30 days consecutively, or five days a week over six weeks or once a week over a whole school year – it's very flexible.

Luke
Jesus' ministry in Galilee
Day/Week 1   pp 1–9
Day/Week 2   pp 9–22
Day/Week 3   pp 23–37
Day/Week 4   pp 37–45
Day/Week 5   pp 45–57

Luke
Jesus' journey to Jerusalem
Day/Week 6   pp 59–68
Day/Week 7   pp 68–77
Day/Week 8   pp 77–85
Day/Week 9   pp 85–93
Day/Week 10   pp 93–102

Luke
Jesus' death and resurrection
Day/Week 11   pp 103–109
Day/Week 12   pp 109–114
Day/Week 13   pp 114–119
Day/Week 14   pp 119–126
Day/Week 15   pp 128–132

Acts
Church established in Jerusalem and beyond
Day/Week 16   pp 135–144
Day/Week 17   pp 144–150
Day/Week 18   pp 150–157
Day/Week 19   pp 159–167
Day/Week 20   pp 167–174

Acts
Gentiles included in church and good news spreads
Day/Week 21   pp 175–188
Day/Week 22   pp 189–197
Day/Week 23   pp 197–206
Day/Week 24   pp 207–213
Day/Week 25   pp 213–220

Acts
Good News about Jesus extended to all nations
Day/Week 26   pp 221–229
Day/Week 27   pp 229–235
Day/Week 28   pp 236–242
Day/Week 29   pp 242–249
Day/Week 30   pp 249–259

5 Questions
to think about when reading *Dear Theo*

No matter how you decide to read *Dear Theo*, involving other people can really help bring the story alive and keep you going to the end. Try to get together once a week to chat about what you're discovering, what questions you have, what you don't understand. The questions below will help with this and are great to think about as you read.

 1. What is something you noticed for the first time?

 2. What questions did you have?

 3. Was there anything that bothered you?

 4. What did you learn about loving God?

 5. What did you learn about loving others?

Extra resources will be available to download from www.biblicaeurope.com/cbe or by contacting us at DearTheo@biblica.com

Dear Theo

Acts

Rome

Asia

Palestine

Europe

Introduction

The story you're about to read was written by a doctor named Luke. Luke wanted his friend Theophilus to know about Jesus, so he wrote a book. Two books, actually: the Gospel of Luke and the book of Acts.

In the first book, God keeps a promise he made to the people of Israel (who were called Jews) by sending Jesus, their long-awaited rescuer and King.

But Jesus also invites non-Jewish people called Gentiles to follow him, because Jesus loves everyone and has come to help them too. This was very good news, especially for Theophilus, who might have been a Gentile himself.

The first book comes in 4 parts:

1. Introduction to the main themes of Luke–Acts telling the story of Jesus' early life (chapter one).
2. Jesus begins his ministry in Galilee, the northern area of the land of Israel (chapter two).
3. Jesus goes on the long journey to Jerusalem, during which he teaches and answers questions about what it means to follow him (chapter three).
4. Jesus gives his life in Jerusalem and then rises

again to be the Ruler and the Saviour of the world (chapter four).

The second book has six parts showing how the community of Jesus' followers expands outward from Jerusalem. Each part ends with a different way of saying, "the word of God continued to spread and flourish".

1. The community of believers is established in Jerusalem and becomes Greek-speaking, enabling it to spread its message throughout the Roman empire (chapter five).
2. The community expands into the rest of Palestine (chapter six).
3. Gentiles are included in the community along with Jews (chapter seven).
4. The community intentionally sends messengers into the Roman province of Asia, which had a large number of people (chapter eight).
5. These messengers enter Europe (chapter nine).
6. The community reaches all the way to the capital of Rome and into the highest levels of society. So, the Good News about Jesus is extended to all nations (chapter ten).

Luke worked hard to make sure he got his facts right. He wanted Theophilus to know he could bet his life on this story. So Luke used many reliable sources. Can you guess what some of them might've been?

Well, there were letters and speeches; songs and travel journals; notes from when people went to court; testimonies from eyewitnesses who knew Jesus; and more.

As you read, remember: this is not just any story. This is the true story of Jesus and his early followers.

♔ One ♔

Many people have attempted to write about the things that have taken place among us. Reports of these things were handed down to us. There were people who saw these things for themselves from the beginning. They saw them and then passed the word on. With this in mind, I myself have carefully looked into everything from the beginning. So I also decided to write down an orderly report of exactly what happened. I am doing this for you, most excellent Theophilus. I want you to know that the things you have been taught are true.

Herod was king of Judea. During the time he was ruling, there was a priest named Zechariah. He belonged to a group of priests named after Abijah. His wife Elizabeth also came from the family line of Aaron. Both of them did what was right in the sight of God. They obeyed all the Lord's commands and rules faithfully. But they had no children, because Elizabeth was not able to have any. And they were both very old.

One day Zechariah's group was on duty. He was serving as a priest in God's temple. He happened to be chosen, in the usual way, to go into the temple of the Lord. There he was supposed to burn incense. The time came for this to be done. All who had gathered to worship were praying outside.

Then an angel of the Lord appeared to Zechariah.

The angel was standing at the right side of the incense altar. When Zechariah saw him, he was amazed and terrified. But the angel said to him, "Do not be afraid, Zechariah. Your prayer has been heard.

Your wife Elizabeth will have a child. It will be a boy, and you must call him John. He will be a joy and delight to you. His birth will make many people very glad. He will be important in the sight of the Lord. He must never drink wine or other such drinks. He will be filled with the Holy Spirit even before he is born. He will bring back many of the people of Israel to the Lord their God. And he will prepare the way for the Lord. He will have the same spirit and power that Elijah had. He will bring peace between parents and their children. He will teach people who don't obey to be wise and do what is right. In this way, he will prepare a people who are ready for the Lord."

Zechariah asked the angel, "How can I be sure of this? I am an old man, and my wife is old too."

The angel said to him, "I am Gabriel. I serve God. I have been sent to speak to you and to tell you this good news. And now you will have to be silent. You will not be able to speak until after John is born. That's because you did not believe my words. They will come true at the time God has chosen."

During that time, the people were waiting for Zechariah to come out of the temple. They wondered why he stayed there so long. When he came out, he could not speak to them. They realised he had seen a vision in the temple. They knew this because he kept gesturing to them. He still could not speak.

When his time of service was over, he returned home. After that, his wife Elizabeth became pregnant. She stayed at home for five months. "The Lord has done this for me," she said. "In these days, he has been kind to me. He has taken away my shame among the people."

In the sixth month after Elizabeth had become pregnant, God sent the angel Gabriel to Nazareth, a town in Galilee. He was sent to a virgin. The girl was engaged to a man named Joseph. He came from the family line of David. The virgin's name was Mary. The angel greeted her and said, "The Lord has blessed you in a special way. He is with you."

Mary was very upset because of his words. She

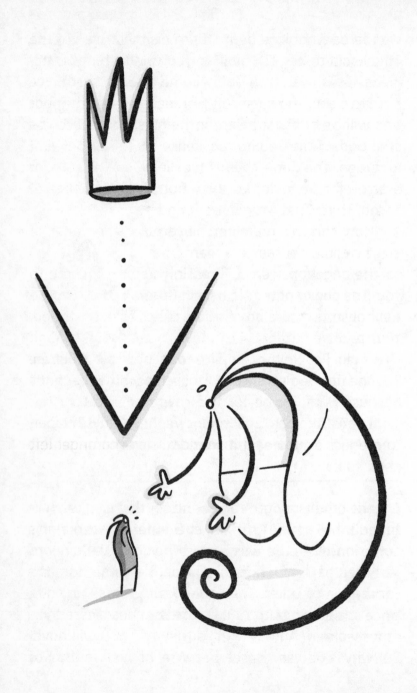

wondered what kind of greeting this could be. But the angel said to her, "Do not be afraid, Mary. God is very pleased with you. You will become pregnant and give birth to a son. You must call him Jesus. He will be great and will be called the Son of the Most High God. The Lord God will make him a king like his father David of long ago. The Son of the Most High God will rule for ever over his people. They are from the family line of Jacob. That kingdom will never end."

"How can this happen?" Mary asked the angel. "I am a virgin."

The angel answered, "The Holy Spirit will come to you. The power of the Most High God will cover you. So the holy one that is born will be called the Son of God. Your relative Elizabeth will have a child even though she is old. People thought she could not have children. But she has been pregnant for six months now. That's because what God says will always come true."

"I serve the Lord," Mary answered. "May it happen to me just as you said it would." Then the angel left her.

At that time Mary got ready and hurried to a town in Judea's hill country. There she entered Zechariah's home and greeted Elizabeth. When Elizabeth heard Mary's greeting, the baby inside her jumped. And Elizabeth was filled with the Holy Spirit. In a loud voice she called out, "God has blessed you more than other women. And blessed is the child you will have! But why is God so kind to me? Why has the mother of my Lord come to me? As soon as I heard the sound of your voice, the baby inside me jumped for joy. You are a woman God has blessed. You have believed that the Lord would keep his promises to you!"

Mary said,

"My soul gives glory to the Lord.
   My spirit delights in God my Saviour.
He has taken note of me
   even though I am not considered important.
From now on all people will call me blessed.
   The Mighty One has done great things
      for me.
   His name is holy.
He shows his mercy to those who have respect
      for him,
   from parent to child down through the years.
He has done mighty things with his powerful
      arm.
   He has scattered those who are proud in
      their deepest thoughts.
He has brought down rulers from their thrones.
   But he has lifted up people who are not
      considered important.
He has filled with good things those who are
      hungry.
   But he has sent away empty those who
      are rich.
He has helped the people of Israel, who
      serve him.
   He has always remembered to be kind

to Abraham and his children down through
   the years.
He has done it just as he promised to our
   people of long ago."

Mary stayed with Elizabeth about three months.
Then she returned home.

The time came for Elizabeth to have her baby. She
gave birth to a son. Her neighbours and relatives heard
that the Lord had been very kind to her. They shared
her joy.

On the eighth day, they came to have the child
circumcised. They were going to name him Zechariah,
like his father. But his mother spoke up. "No!" she said.
"He must be called John."

They said to her, "No-one among your relatives has
that name."

Then they motioned to his father. They wanted
to find out what he would like to name the child. He
asked for something to write on. Then he wrote, "His
name is John." Everyone was amazed. Right away
Zechariah could speak again. Right away he praised
God. All his neighbours were filled with fear and
wonder. Throughout Judea's hill country, people were
talking about all these things. Everyone who heard this
wondered about it. And because the Lord was with
John, they asked, "What is this child going to be?"

John's father Zechariah was filled with the Holy
Spirit. He prophesied,

"Give praise to the Lord, the God of Israel!
  He has come to his people and purchased
        their freedom.
He has acted with great power and has
        saved us.
  He did it for those who are from the family
        line of his servant David.
Long ago holy prophets said he would
        do it.
He has saved us from our enemies.
  We are rescued from all who hate us.
He has been kind to our people of long ago.
  He has remembered his holy covenant.
  He made a promise to our father
        Abraham.
He promised to save us from our enemies.
  Then we could serve him without fear.
  He wants us to be holy and godly as long as
        we live.

"And you, my child, will be called a prophet of
        the Most High God.
  You will go ahead of the Lord to prepare the
        way for him.
You will tell his people how they can be saved.
  You will tell them that their sins can be
        forgiven.
All of that will happen because our God is
        tender and caring.
  His kindness will bring the rising sun to us
        from heaven.

It will shine on those living in darkness
  and in the shadow of death.
It will guide our feet on the path
    of peace."

The child grew up,
and his spirit
became
strong. He
lived in the desert until
he appeared openly to Israel.

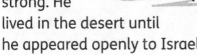

In those days, Caesar Augustus made a law. It required that a list be made of everyone in the whole Roman world. It was the first time a list was made of the

people while Quirinius was governor of Syria. Everyone went to their own town to be listed.

So Joseph went also. He went from the town of Nazareth in Galilee to Judea. That is where Bethlehem, the town of David, was. Joseph went there because he belonged to the family line of David. He went there with Mary to be listed. Mary was engaged to him. She was expecting a baby. While Joseph and Mary were there, the time came for the child to be born. She gave birth to her first baby. It was a boy. She wrapped him in large strips of cloth. Then she placed him in a manger. That's because there was no guest room where they could stay.

There were shepherds living out in the fields nearby. It was night, and they were taking care of their sheep. An angel of the Lord appeared to them. And the glory of the Lord shone around them. They were terrified. But the angel said to them, "Do not be afraid. I bring you good news. It will bring great joy for all the people. Today in the town of David a Saviour has been born to you. He is the Messiah, the Lord. Here is how you will know I am telling you the truth. You will find a baby wrapped in strips of cloth and lying in a manger."

Suddenly a large group of angels from heaven also appeared. They were praising God. They said,

"May glory be given to God in the highest
        heaven!
And may peace be given to those he is
        pleased with on earth!"

The angels left and went into heaven. Then the shepherds said to one another, "Let's go to Bethlehem. Let's see this thing that has happened, which the Lord has told us about."

So they hurried off and found Mary and Joseph and the baby. The baby was lying in the manger. After the shepherds had seen him, they told everyone. They reported what the angel had said about this child. All who heard it were amazed at what the shepherds said to them. But Mary kept all these things like a secret treasure in her heart. She thought about them over and over. The shepherds returned. They gave glory and praise to God. Everything they had seen and heard was just as they had been told.

When the child was eight days old, he was circumcised. At the same time he was named Jesus. This was the name the angel had given him before his mother became pregnant.

The time came for making Mary "clean" as required by the Law of Moses. So Joseph and Mary took Jesus to Jerusalem. There they presented him to the Lord. In the Law of the Lord it says, "The first boy born in every family must be set apart for the Lord." *(from the Book of Exodus)* They also offered a sacrifice. They did it in keeping with the Law, which says, "a pair of doves or two young pigeons." *(from the Book of Leviticus)*

In Jerusalem there was a man named Simeon. He was a good and godly man. He was waiting for God's promise to Israel to come true. The Holy Spirit was with him. The Spirit had told Simeon that he would not die before he had seen the Lord's Messiah. The Spirit led him into the temple courtyard. Then Jesus' parents brought the child in. They came to do for him what the Law required. Simeon took Jesus in his arms and praised God. He said,

"Lord, you are the King over all.
  Now let me, your servant,
      go in peace.
  That is what you promised.
My eyes have seen your
      salvation.
  You have prepared it in
      the sight of all
      nations.
It is a light to be given to
      the Gentiles.
  It will be the glory
      of your people
      Israel."

The child's father and mother were amazed at what was said about him. Then Simeon blessed them. He said to Mary, Jesus' mother, "This child is going to cause many people in

Israel to fall and to rise. God has sent him. But many will speak against him. The thoughts of many hearts will be known. A sword will wound your own soul too."

There was also a prophet named Anna. She was the daughter of Penuel from the tribe of Asher. Anna was very old. After getting married, she lived with her husband seven years. Then she was a widow until she was 84. She never left the temple. She worshipped night and day, praying and going without food. Anna came up to Jesus' family at that moment. She gave thanks to God. And she spoke about the child to all who were looking forward to the time when Jerusalem would be set free.

Joseph and Mary did everything the Law of the Lord required. Then they returned to Galilee. They went to their own town of Nazareth. And the child grew and became strong. He was very wise. He was blessed by God's grace.

Every year Jesus' parents went to Jerusalem for the Passover Feast. When Jesus was 12 years old, they went up to the feast as usual. After the feast was over, his parents left to go back home. The boy Jesus stayed behind in Jerusalem. But they were not aware of it. They thought he was somewhere in their group. So they travelled on for a day. Then they began to look for him among their relatives and friends. They did not find him. So they went back to Jerusalem to look for him. After three days they found him in the temple courtyard. He was sitting with the teachers. He was listening to them and asking them questions. Everyone who heard him was amazed at how much he understood. They also were amazed at his answers. When his parents saw him, they were amazed. His mother said to him, "Son, why have you treated us like this? Your father and I have been worried about you. We have been looking for you everywhere."

"Why were you looking for me?" he asked. "Didn't you know I had to be in my Father's house?" But they did not understand what he meant by that.

Then he went back to Nazareth with them, and he obeyed them. But his mother kept all these things like a secret treasure in her heart. Jesus became wiser and stronger. He also became more and more pleasing to God and to people.

Tiberius Caesar had been ruling for 15 years. Pontius Pilate was governor of Judea. Herod was the ruler of Galilee. His brother Philip was the ruler of Iturea and Traconitis. Lysanias was ruler of Abilene. Annas and Caiaphas were high priests. At that time God's word came to John, son of Zechariah, in the desert. He went into all the countryside around the River Jordan.

There he preached that people should be baptised and turn away from their sins. Then God would forgive them. Here is what is written in the book of Isaiah the prophet. It says,

> "A messenger is calling out in the desert,
> 'Prepare the way for the Lord.
>   Make straight paths for him.
> Every valley will be filled in.
>   Every mountain and hill will be made level.
> The crooked roads will become straight.
>   The rough ways will become smooth.
> And all people will see God's salvation.'"

(from the prophet Isaiah)

John spoke to the crowds coming to be baptised by him. He said, "You are like a nest of poisonous snakes! Who warned you to escape the coming of God's anger? Live in a way that shows you have turned away from your sins. And don't start saying to yourselves, 'Abraham is our father.' I tell you, God can raise up children for Abraham even from these stones. The axe is already lying at the roots of the trees. All the trees that don't produce good fruit will be cut down. They will be thrown into the fire."

"Then what should we do?" the crowd asked.

John answered, "Anyone who has extra clothes should share with the one who has none. And anyone who has extra food should do the same."

Even tax collectors came to be baptised. "Teacher," they asked, "what should we do?"

"Don't collect any more than you are required to," John told them.

Then some soldiers asked him, "And what should we do?"

John replied, "Don't force people to give you money. Don't bring false charges against people. Be happy with your pay."

The people were waiting. They were expecting something. They were all wondering in their hearts if John might be the Messiah. John answered them all, "I baptise you with water. But one who is more powerful than I am will come. I'm not good enough to untie the straps of his sandals. He will baptise you with the Holy Spirit and fire. His pitchfork is in his hand to toss the straw away from his threshing floor. He will gather the wheat into his barn. But he will burn the husks with fire that can't be put out." John said many other things to warn the people. He also announced the good news to them.

But John found fault with Herod, the ruler of Galilee, because of his marriage to Herodias. She was the wife of Herod's brother. John also spoke strongly to Herod about all the other evil things he had done. So Herod locked John up in prison. Herod added this sin to all his others.

When all the people were being baptised, Jesus was baptised too. And as he was praying, heaven was opened. The Holy Spirit came to rest on him in the form

of a dove. A voice came from heaven. It said, "You are my Son, and I love you. I am very pleased with you."

Jesus was about 30 years old when he began his special work for God and others. It was thought that he was the son of Joseph.

Joseph was the son of Heli.
Heli was the son of Matthat.
Matthat was the son of Levi.
Levi was the son of Melki.
Melki was the son of Jannai.
Jannai was the son of Joseph.
Joseph was the son of Mattathias.
Mattathias was the son of Amos.
Amos was the son of Nahum.

Nahum was the son of Esli.
Esli was the son of Naggai.
Naggai was the son of Maath.
Maath was the son of Mattathias.
Mattathias was the son of Semein.
Semein was the son of Josek.
Josek was the son of Joda.
Joda was the son of Joanan.
Joanan was the son of Rhesa.
Rhesa was the son of Zerubbabel.
Zerubbabel was the son of Shealtiel.
Shealtiel was the son of Neri.
Neri was the son of Melki.
Melki was the son of Addi.
Addi was the son of Cosam.
Cosam was the son of Elmadam.
Elmadam was the son of Er.
Er was the son of Joshua.
Joshua was the son of Eliezer.
Eliezer was the son of Jorim.
Jorim was the son of Matthat.
Matthat was the son of Levi.
Levi was the son of Simeon.
Simeon was the son of Judah.
Judah was the son of Joseph.
Joseph was the son of Jonam.
Jonam was the son of Eliakim.
Eliakim was the son of Melea.
Melea was the son of Menna.

Menna was the son of Mattatha.
Mattatha was the son of Nathan.
Nathan was the son of David.
David was the son of Jesse.
Jesse was the son of Obed.
Obed was the son of Boaz.
Boaz was the son of Salmon.
Salmon was the son of Nahshon.
Nahshon was the son of Amminadab.
Amminadab was the son of Ram.
Ram was the son of Hezron.
Hezron was the son of Perez.
Perez was the son of Judah.
Judah was the son of Jacob.
Jacob was the son of Isaac.
Isaac was the son of Abraham.
Abraham was the son of Terah.
Terah was the son of Nahor.
Nahor was the son of Serug.
Serug was the son of Reu.
Reu was the son of Peleg.
Peleg was the son of Eber.
Eber was the son of Shelah.
Shelah was the son of Cainan.
Cainan was the son of Arphaxad.
Arphaxad was the son of Shem.
Shem was the son of Noah.
Noah was the son of Lamech.
Lamech was the son of Methuselah.
Methuselah was the son of Enoch.

Enoch was the son of Jared.
Jared was the son of Mahalalel.
Mahalalel was the son of Kenan.
Kenan was the son of Enosh.
Enosh was the son of Seth.
Seth was the son of Adam.
Adam was the son of God.

Jesus, full of the Holy Spirit, left the River Jordan. The Spirit led him into the desert. There the devil tempted him for 40 days. Jesus ate nothing during that time. At the end of the 40 days, he was hungry.

The devil said to him, "If you are the Son of God, tell this stone to become bread."

Jesus answered, "It is written, 'Man must not live only on bread.'" *(from the Book of Deuteronomy)*

Then the devil led Jesus up to a high place. In an instant, he showed Jesus all the kingdoms of the world. He said to Jesus, "I will give you all their authority and glory. It has been given to me, and I can give it to anyone I want to. If you worship me, it will all be yours."

Jesus answered, "It is written, 'Worship the Lord your God. He is the only one you should serve.'" *(from the Book of Deuteronomy)*

Then the devil led Jesus to Jerusalem. He had Jesus stand on the highest point of the temple. "If you are the Son of God," he said, "throw yourself down from here. It is written,

"'The Lord will command his angels to take
          good care of you.
They will lift you up in their hands.
          Then you won't trip over a stone.'" *(from Psalm 91)*

Jesus answered, "Scripture says, 'Do not test the Lord your God.'" *(from the Book of Deuteronomy)*

When the devil finished all this tempting, he left Jesus until a better time.

♕ Two ♕

Jesus returned to Galilee in the power of the Holy Spirit. News about him spread through the whole countryside. He was teaching in their synagogues, and everyone praised him.

Jesus went to Nazareth, where he had been brought up. On the Sabbath day he went into the synagogue as he usually did. He stood up to read. And the scroll of Isaiah the prophet was handed to him. Jesus unrolled it and found the right place. There it is written,

"The Spirit of the Lord
is on me.
He has anointed me
to announce the
good news to poor people.
He has sent me to announce freedom for
prisoners.
He has sent me so that the blind will see
again.
He wants me to set free those who are treated
badly.
And he has sent me to announce the year
when he will set his people free."

(from the prophet Isaiah)

4:14–4:19

Then Jesus rolled up the scroll. He gave it back to the attendant and sat down. The eyes of everyone in the synagogue were staring at him. He began by saying to them, "Today this passage of Scripture is coming true as you listen."

Everyone said good things about him. They were amazed at the gracious words they heard from his lips. "Isn't this Joseph's son?" they asked.

Jesus said, "Here is a saying you will certainly apply to me. 'Doctor, heal yourself!' And you will tell me this. 'Do the things here in your home town that we heard you did in Capernaum.'"

"What I'm about to tell you is true," he continued. "A prophet is not accepted in his home town. I tell you for sure that there were many widows in Israel in the days of Elijah. And there had been no rain for three and a half years. There wasn't enough food to eat anywhere in the land. But Elijah was not sent to any of those widows. Instead, he was sent to a widow in Zarephath near Sidon. And there were many in Israel who had skin diseases in the days of Elisha the prophet. But not one of them was healed except Naaman the Syrian."

All the people in the synagogue were very angry when they heard that. They got up and ran Jesus out of town. They took him to the edge of the hill on which the town was built. They planned to throw him off the cliff. But Jesus walked right through the crowd and went on his way.

Then Jesus went to Capernaum, a town in Galilee.

On the Sabbath day he taught the people. They were amazed at his teaching, because his words had authority.

In the synagogue there was a man controlled by a demon, an evil spirit. He cried out at the top of his voice. "Go away!" he said. "What do you want with us, Jesus of Nazareth? Have you come to destroy us? I know who you are. You are the Holy One of God!"

"Be quiet!" Jesus said firmly. "Come out of him!" Then the demon threw the man down in front of everybody. And it came out without hurting him.

All the people were amazed. They said to each other, "What he says is amazing! With authority and power he gives orders to evil spirits. And they come out!" The news about Jesus spread throughout the whole area.

Jesus left the synagogue and went to the home of Simon. At that time, Simon's mother in law was suffering from a high fever. So they asked Jesus to help her. He bent over her and commanded the fever to leave, and it left her. She got up right away and began to serve them.

At sunset, people brought to Jesus all who were ill. He placed his hands on each one and healed them. Also, demons came out of many people. The demons shouted, "You are the Son of God!" But he commanded them to be quiet. He would not allow them to speak, because they knew he was the Messiah.

At dawn, Jesus went out to a place where he could

be by himself. The people went to look for him. When they found him, they tried to keep him from leaving them. But he said, "I must announce the good news of God's kingdom to the other towns also. That is why I was sent." And he kept on preaching in the synagogues of Judea.

One day Jesus was standing by the Sea of Galilee. The people crowded around him and listened to the word of God. Jesus saw two boats at the edge of the water. They had been left there by the fishermen, who were washing their nets. He got into the boat that belonged to Simon. Jesus asked him to go out a little way from shore. Then he sat down in the boat and taught the people.

When he finished speaking, he turned to Simon. Jesus said, "Go out into deep water. Let down the nets so you can catch some fish."

Simon answered, "Master, we've worked hard all night and haven't caught anything. But because you say so, I will let down the nets."

When they had done so, they caught a large number of fish. There were so many that their nets began to break. So they motioned to their partners in the other boat to come and help them. They came and filled both boats so full that they began to sink.

When Simon Peter saw this, he fell at Jesus' knees. "Go away from me, Lord!" he said. "I am a sinful man!" He and everyone with him were amazed at the number of fish they had caught. So were James and John, the sons of Zebedee, who worked with Simon.

Then Jesus said to Simon, "Don't be afraid. From now on you will fish for people." So they pulled their boats up on shore. Then they left everything and followed him.

While Jesus was in one of the towns, a man came along. He had a skin disease all over his body. When he saw Jesus, the man fell with his face to the ground. He begged him, "Lord, if you are willing to make me 'clean', you can do it."

Jesus reached out his hand and touched the man. "I am willing to do it," he said. "Be 'clean'!" Right away the disease left him.

Then Jesus ordered him, "Don't tell anyone. Go and show yourself to the priest. Offer the sacrifices that Moses commanded. It will be a witness to the priest and the people that you are 'clean'."

But the news about Jesus spread even more. So crowds of people came to hear him. They also came to be healed of their diseases. But Jesus often went away to be by himself and pray.

One day Jesus was teaching.

Pharisees and teachers of the law were sitting there. They had come from every village of Galilee and from Judea and Jerusalem. They heard that the Lord had given Jesus the power to heal the ill. So some men came carrying a man who could not walk. He was lying on a mat. They tried to take him into the house to place him in front of Jesus. They could not find a way to do this because of the crowd. So they went up on the roof. Then they lowered the man on his mat through the opening in the roof tiles. They lowered him into the middle of the crowd, right in front of Jesus.

When Jesus saw that they had faith, he spoke to the man. He said, "Friend, your sins are forgiven."

The Pharisees and the teachers of the law began to think, "Who is this fellow who says such an evil thing? Who can forgive sins but God alone?"

Jesus knew what they were thinking. So he asked, "Why are you thinking these things in your hearts? Is it easier to say, 'Your sins are forgiven'? Or to say, 'Get up and walk'? But I want you to know that the Son of Man has authority on earth to forgive sins." So he spoke to the man who could not walk. "I tell you," he said, "get up. Take your mat and go home." Right away, the man stood up in front of them. He took his mat and went home praising God. Everyone was amazed and gave praise to God. They were filled with wonder. They said, "We have seen unusual things today."

After this, Jesus left the house. He saw a tax collector sitting at the tax booth. The man's name was Levi.

"Follow me," Jesus said to him. Levi got up, left everything and followed him.

Then Levi gave a huge banquet for Jesus at his house. A large crowd of tax collectors and others were eating with them. But the Pharisees and their teachers of the law complained to Jesus' disciples. They said, "Why do you eat and drink with tax collectors and sinners?"

Jesus answered them, "Healthy people don't need a doctor. Ill people do. I have not come to get those who think they are right with God to follow me. I have come to get sinners to turn away from their sins."

Some of the people who were there said to Jesus, "John's disciples often pray and go without eating. So do the disciples of the Pharisees. But yours go on eating and drinking."

Jesus answered, "Can you make the friends of the groom fast while he is with them? But the time will come when the groom will be taken away from them. In those days they will go without eating."

Then Jesus gave them an example. He said, "No-one tears a piece out of new clothes to patch old clothes. Otherwise, they will tear the new clothes. Also, the patch from the new clothes will not match the old clothes. No-one pours new wine into old wineskins. Otherwise, the new wine will burst the skins. The wine will run out, and the wineskins will be destroyed. No, new wine must be poured into new wineskins. After drinking old wine, no-one wants the new. They say, 'The old wine is better.'"

One Sabbath day Jesus was walking through the cornfields. His disciples began to break off some ears of corn. They rubbed them in their hands and ate them. Some of the Pharisees said, "It is against the Law to do this on the Sabbath day. Why are you doing it?"

Jesus answered them, "Haven't you ever read about what David did? He and his men were hungry. He entered the house of God and took the holy bread. He ate the bread that only priests were allowed to eat. David also gave some to his men." Then Jesus said to them, "The Son of Man is Lord of the Sabbath day."

On another Sabbath day, Jesus went into the synagogue and was teaching. A man whose right hand was weak and twisted was there. The Pharisees and the teachers of the law were trying to find fault with Jesus. So they watched him closely. They wanted to see if he would heal on the Sabbath day. But Jesus knew what they were thinking. He spoke to the man who had the weak and twisted hand. "Get up and stand in front of everyone," he said. So the man got up and stood there.

Then Jesus said to them, "What does the Law say we should do on the Sabbath day? Should we do good? Or should we do evil? Should we save life? Or should we destroy it?"

He looked around at all of them. Then he said to the man, "Stretch out your hand." He did, and his hand had been made as good as new. But the Pharisees and the teachers of the law were very angry. They began to talk to one another about what they might do to Jesus.

On one of those days, Jesus went out to a mountainside to pray. He spent the night praying to God. When morning came, he called for his disciples to come to him. He chose 12 of them and made them apostles.

Simon, whom Jesus named Peter, and his brother Andrew
James
John
Philip
Bartholomew
Matthew
Thomas
James, son of Alphaeus
Simon who was called the Zealot
Judas, son of James
and Judas Iscariot who would later hand Jesus over to his enemies

Jesus went down the mountain with them and stood on a level place. A large crowd of his disciples

was there. A large number of other people were there too. They came from all over Judea, including Jerusalem. They also came from the coastland around Tyre and Sidon. They had all come to hear Jesus and to be healed of their diseases. People who were troubled by evil spirits were made well. Everyone tried to touch Jesus. Power was coming from him and healing them all.

Jesus looked at his disciples. He said to them,

"Blessed are you who are needy.
    God's kingdom belongs to you.
Blessed are you who are hungry now.
    You will be satisfied.
Blessed are you who are sad now.
    You will laugh.
Blessed are you when people hate you,
    when they have nothing to do with you
    and say bad things about you,
    and when they treat your name as
       something evil.
       They do all this because you are followers
       of the Son of Man.

"The prophets of long ago were treated the same way. When these things happen to you, be glad and jump for joy. You will receive many blessings in heaven.

"But how terrible it will be for you who are rich!
 You have already had your easy life.
How terrible for you who are well fed now!
 You will go hungry.
How terrible for you who laugh now!
 You will cry and be sad.
How terrible for you when everyone says good
  things about you!
 Their people treated the false prophets the
  same way long ago.

"But here is what I tell you who are listening. Love your enemies. Do good to those who hate you. Bless those who call down curses on you. And pray for those who treat you badly. Suppose someone slaps you on one cheek. Let them slap you on the other cheek as well. Suppose someone takes your coat. Don't stop them from taking your shirt as well. Give to everyone who asks you. And if anyone takes what belongs to you, don't ask to get it back. Do to others as you want them to do to you.

"Suppose you love those who love you. Should anyone praise you for that? Even sinners love those who love them. And suppose you do good to those who are good to you. Should anyone praise you for that? Even sinners do that. And suppose you lend money to those who can pay you back. Should anyone praise you for that? Even a sinner lends to sinners, expecting them to pay everything back. But love your enemies. Do good to them. Lend to them without expecting to get anything back. Then you will receive a lot in return. And you will be children of the Most High God. He is kind to people who are evil and are not thankful. So have mercy, just as your Father has mercy.

"If you do not judge other people, then you will not be judged. If you do not find others guilty, then you will not be found guilty. Forgive, and you will be forgiven. Give, and it will be given to you. A good amount will be poured into your lap. It will be pressed down, shaken together, and running over. The same amount you give will be measured out to you."

Jesus also gave them another example. He asked, "Can a blind person lead another blind person? Won't they both fall into a pit? The student is not better than the teacher. But everyone who is completely trained will be like their teacher.

"You look at the bit of sawdust in your friend's eye. But you pay no attention to the piece of wood in your own eye. How can you say to your friend, 'Let me take the bit of sawdust out of your eye'? How can you say this while there is a piece of wood in your own eye? You pretender! First take the piece of wood out of your own eye. Then you will be able to see clearly to take the bit of sawdust out of your friend's eye.

"A good tree doesn't bear bad fruit. And a bad tree doesn't bear good fruit. You can tell each tree

by the kind of fruit it bears. People do not pick figs from thorns. And they don't pick grapes from bushes. A good man says good things. These come from the good that is stored up in his heart. An evil man says evil things. These come from the evil that is stored up in his heart. A person's mouth says everything that is in their heart.

"Why do you call me, 'Lord, Lord', and still don't do what I say? Some people come and listen to me and do what I say. I will show you what they are like. They are like a man who builds a house. He digs down deep and sets it on solid rock. When a flood comes, the river rushes against the house. But the water can't shake it. The house is well built. But here is what happens when

people listen to my words and do not obey them. They are like a man who builds a house on soft ground instead of solid rock. The moment the river rushes against that house, it falls down. It is completely destroyed."

Jesus finished saying all these things to the people who were listening. Then he entered Capernaum. There the servant of a Roman commander was ill and about to die. His master thought highly of him. The commander heard about Jesus. So he sent some elders of the Jews to him. He told them to ask Jesus to come and heal his servant. They came to Jesus and begged him, "This man deserves to have you do this. He loves our nation and has built our synagogue." So Jesus went with them.

When Jesus came near the house, the Roman commander sent friends to him. He told them to say, "Lord, don't trouble yourself. I am not good enough to have you come into my house. That is why I did not even think I was fit to come to you. But just say the word, and my servant will be healed. I myself am a man who is under authority. And I have soldiers who obey my orders. I tell this one, 'Go', and he goes. I tell that one, 'Come', and he comes. I say to my servant, 'Do this', and he does it."

When Jesus heard this, he was amazed at the commander. Jesus turned to the crowd that was following him. He said, "I tell you, even in Israel I have not found anyone whose faith is so strong." Then the men who had been sent to Jesus returned to the house. They found that the servant was healed.

Some time later, Jesus went to a town called Nain. His disciples and a large crowd went along with him. He approached the town gate. Just then, a dead person was being carried out. He was the only son of his mother. She was a widow. A large crowd from the town was with her. When the Lord saw her, he felt sorry for her. So he said, "Don't cry."

Then he went up and touched the coffin. Those carrying it stood still. Jesus said, "Young man, I say to you, get up!" The dead man sat up and began to talk. Then Jesus gave him back to his mother.

The people were all filled with wonder and praised God. "A great prophet has appeared among us," they said. "God has come to help his people." This news about Jesus spread all through Judea and the whole country.

John's disciples told him about all these things. So he chose two of them. He sent them to the Lord. John told them to ask him, "Are you the one who is supposed to come? Or should we look for someone else?"

The men came to Jesus. They said, "John the Baptist sent us to ask you, 'Are you the one who is supposed to come? Or should we look for someone else?'"

At that time Jesus healed many people. They had illnesses, diseases and evil spirits. He also gave sight to many who were blind. So Jesus replied to the messengers, "Go back to John. Tell him what you have seen and heard. Blind people receive sight. Disabled people walk. Those who have skin diseases are made 'clean'. Deaf people hear. Those who are dead are raised to life. And the good news is announced to those who are poor. Blessed is anyone who does not give up their faith because of me."

So John's messengers left. Then Jesus began to speak to the crowd about John. He said, "What did you go out into the desert to see? Tall grass waving in the wind? If not, what did you go out to see? A man dressed in fine clothes? No. Those who wear fine clothes and have many expensive things are in palaces. Then what did you go out to see? A prophet? Yes, I tell you, and more than a prophet. He is the one written about in Scripture. It says,

> "'I will send my messenger ahead of you.
>   He will prepare your way for you.'

> *(from the prophet Malachi)*

I tell you, no-one more important than John has ever been born. But the least important person in God's kingdom is more important than John is."

All the people who heard Jesus' words agreed that God's way was right. Even the tax collectors agreed.

These people had all been baptised by John. But the Pharisees and the authorities on the law did not accept for themselves God's purpose. So they had not been baptised by John.

Jesus went on to say, "What can I compare today's people to? What are they like? They are like children sitting in the market and calling out to each other. They say,

"'We played the flute for you.
    But you didn't dance.
We sang a funeral song.
    But you didn't cry.'

"That is how it has been with John the Baptist. When he came to you, he didn't eat bread or drink wine. And you say, 'He has a demon.' But when the Son of Man came, he ate and drank as you do. And you say, 'This fellow is always eating and drinking far too much. He's a friend of tax collectors and sinners.' All who follow wisdom prove that wisdom is right."

One of the Pharisees invited Jesus to have dinner with him. So he went to the Pharisee's house. He took his place at the table. There was a woman in that town who had lived a sinful life. She learned that Jesus was eating at the Pharisee's house. So she came there with a special jar of perfume. She stood behind Jesus and cried at his feet. And she began to wet his feet with her tears. Then she wiped them with her hair. She kissed them and poured perfume on them.

The Pharisee who had invited Jesus saw this. He said to himself, "If this man were a prophet, he would know who is touching him. He would know what kind of woman she is. She is a sinner!"

Jesus answered him, "Simon, I have something to tell you."

"Tell me, teacher," he said.

"Two people owed money to a certain lender. One owed him 500 silver coins. The other owed him 50 silver coins. Neither of them had the money to pay him back. So he let them go without paying. Which of them will love him more?"

Simon replied, "I suppose the one who owed the most money."

"You are right," Jesus said.

Then he turned towards the woman. He said to Simon, "Do you see this woman? I came into your house. You did not give me any water to wash my feet. But she wet my feet with her tears and wiped them with her hair. You did not give me a kiss. But this woman has not stopped kissing my feet since I came in. You did not put any olive oil on my head. But she has poured this perfume on my feet. So I tell you this. Her many sins have been forgiven. She has shown that she understands this by her great acts of love. But whoever who has been forgiven only a little loves only a little."

Then Jesus said to her, "Your sins are forgiven."

The other guests began to talk about this among themselves. They said, "Who is this who even forgives sins?"

Jesus said to the woman, "Your faith has saved you. Go in peace."

After this, Jesus travelled around from one town and village to another. He announced the good news of God's kingdom. His 12 disciples were with him. So were some women who had been healed of evil spirits and diseases. One was Mary Magdalene. Seven demons had come out of her. Another was Joanna, the wife of Chuza. He was the manager of Herod's household. Susanna and many others were there also. These women were helping to support Jesus and the 12 disciples with their own money.

A large crowd gathered together. People came to Jesus from town after town. As they did, he told a story. He said, "A farmer went out to plant his seed. He scattered the seed on the ground. Some fell on a path. People walked on it, and the birds ate it up. Some seed fell on rocky ground. When it grew, the plants dried up because they had no water. Other seed fell among thorns. The thorns grew up with it and crowded out the plants. Still other seed fell on good soil. It grew up and produced a crop 100 times more than the farmer planted."

When Jesus said this, he called out, "Whoever has ears should listen."

His disciples asked him what the story meant. He said, "You have been given the chance to understand the secrets of God's kingdom. But to outsiders I speak by using stories. In that way,

" 'They see, but they will not know what they
    are seeing.
They hear, but they will not understand what
    they are hearing.'   *(from the prophet Isaiah)*

"Here is what the story means. The seed is God's message. The seed on the path stands for God's message in the hearts of those who hear. But then the devil comes. He takes away the message from their hearts. He does it so they won't believe. Then they can't be saved. The seed on rocky ground stands for those who hear the message and receive it with joy. But they have no roots. They believe for a while. But when they are tested, they fall away from the faith. The seed that fell among thorns stands for those who hear the message. But as they go on their way, they are choked by life's worries, riches and pleasures. So they do not reach full growth. But the seed on good soil stands for those with an honest and good heart. Those people hear the message. They keep it in their hearts. They remain faithful and produce a good crop.

"No-one lights a lamp and then hides it in a clay jar or puts it under a bed. Instead, they put it on a stand. Then those who come in can see its light. What is hidden will be seen. And what is out of sight will be brought into the open and made known.

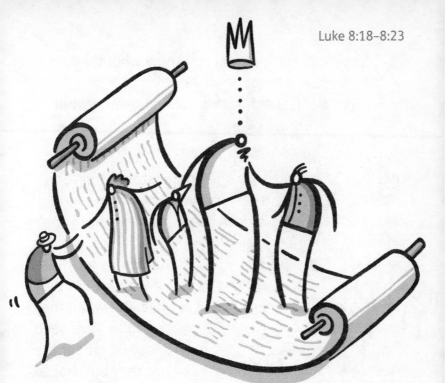

So be careful how you listen. Whoever has something will be given more. Whoever has nothing, even what they think they have will be taken away from them."

Jesus' mother and brothers came to see him. But they could not get near him because of the crowd. Someone told him, "Your mother and brothers are standing outside. They want to see you."

He replied, "My mother and brothers are those who hear God's word and do what it says."

One day Jesus said to his disciples, "Let's go over to the other side of the lake." So they got into a boat and left. As they sailed, Jesus fell asleep. A storm came down

on the lake. It was so bad that the boat was about to sink. They were in great danger.

The disciples went and woke Jesus up. They said, "Master! Master! We're going to drown!"

He got up and ordered the wind and the huge waves to stop. The storm quietened down. It was completely calm. "Where is your faith?" he asked his disciples.

They were amazed and full of fear. They asked one another, "Who is this? He commands even the winds and the waves, and they obey him."

Jesus and his disciples sailed to the area of the Gerasenes across the lake from Galilee. When Jesus stepped on shore, he was met by a man from the town. The man was controlled by demons. For a long time he had not worn clothes or lived in a house. He lived in the tombs. When he saw Jesus, he cried out and fell at his feet. He shouted at the top of his voice, "Jesus, Son of the Most High God, what do you want with me? I beg you, don't hurt me!" This was because Jesus had commanded the evil spirit to come out of the man. Many times the spirit had taken hold of him. The man's hands and feet were chained, and he was kept under guard. But he had broken his chains. And then the demon had forced him to go out into lonely places in the countryside.

Jesus asked him, "What is your name?"

"Legion," he replied, because many demons had gone into him. And they begged Jesus again and again not to order them to go into the Abyss.

A large herd of pigs was feeding there on the hillside. The demons begged Jesus to let them go into the pigs. And he allowed it. When the demons came out of the man, they went into the pigs. Then the herd rushed down the steep bank. They ran into the lake and drowned.

Those who were tending the pigs saw what had happened. They ran off and reported it in the town and countryside. The people went out to see what had happened. Then they came to Jesus. They found the man who was now free of the demons. He was sitting at Jesus' feet. He was dressed and thinking clearly. All this made the people afraid. Those who had seen it told the others how the man who had been controlled by demons was now healed. Then all the people who lived in the area of the Gerasenes asked Jesus to leave them. They were filled with fear. So he got into the boat and left.

The man who was now free of the demons begged to go with him. But Jesus sent him away. He said to him, "Return home and tell how much God has done for you." So the man went away. He told people all over town how much Jesus had done for him.

When Jesus returned, a crowd welcomed him. They were all expecting him. Then a man named Jairus came. He was a synagogue leader. He fell at Jesus' feet and begged Jesus to come to his house. His only daughter was dying. She was about 12 years old. As Jesus was on his way, the crowds almost crushed him.

A woman was there who had a sickness that made her bleed. Her sickness had lasted for 12 years. No-one could heal her. She came up behind Jesus and touched the edge of his clothes. Right away her bleeding stopped.

"Who touched me?" Jesus asked.

Everyone said they didn't do it. Then Peter said, "Master, the people are crowding and pushing against you."

But Jesus said, "Someone touched me. I know that power has gone out from me."

The woman realised that people would notice her. Shaking with fear, she came and fell at his feet. In front of everyone, she told why she had touched him. She also told how she had been healed in an instant. Then he said to her, "Dear woman, your faith has healed you. Go in peace."

While Jesus was still speaking, someone came from the house of Jairus. Jairus was the synagogue leader. "Your daughter is dead," the messenger said. "Don't bother the teacher anymore."

Hearing this, Jesus said to Jairus, "Don't be afraid. Just believe. She will be healed."

When he arrived at the house of Jairus, he did not let everyone go in with him. He took only Peter, John and James, and the child's father and mother. During this time, all the people were crying and sobbing loudly over the child. "Stop crying!" Jesus said. "She is not dead. She is sleeping."

They laughed at him. They knew she was dead. But

he took her by the hand and said, "My child, get up!" Her spirit returned, and right away she stood up. Then Jesus told them to give her something to eat. Her parents were amazed. But Jesus ordered them not to tell anyone what had happened.

Jesus called together the 12 disciples. He gave them power and authority to drive out all demons and to heal diseases. Then he sent them out to announce God's kingdom and to heal those who were ill. He told them, "Don't take anything for the journey. Do not take a walking stick or a bag. Do not take any bread, money or extra clothes. When you are invited into a house, stay there until you leave town. Some people may not welcome you. If they don't, leave their town and shake the dust off your feet. This will be a witness against the people living there."

So the 12 disciples left. They went from village to village. They announced the good news and healed people everywhere.

Now Herod, the ruler of Galilee, heard about everything that was going on. He was bewildered, because some were saying that John the Baptist had been raised from the dead. Others were saying that Elijah had appeared. Still others were saying that a prophet of long ago had come back to life. But Herod said, "I had John's head cut off. So who is it that I hear such things about?" And he tried to see Jesus.

The disciples returned. They told Jesus what they had done. Then he took them with him. They went off by themselves to a town called Bethsaida. But the crowds learned about it and followed Jesus. He welcomed them and spoke to them about God's kingdom. He also healed those who needed to be healed.

Late in the afternoon the 12 disciples came to him. They said, "Send the crowd away. They can go to the nearby villages and countryside. There they can find food and a place to stay. There is nothing here."

Jesus replied, "You give them something to eat."

The disciples answered, "We have only five loaves of bread and two fish. We would have to go and buy food for all this crowd." About 5,000 men were there.

But Jesus said to his disciples, "Have them sit down in groups of about 50 each." The disciples did so, and everyone sat down. Jesus took the five loaves and the two fish. He looked up to heaven and gave thanks. He broke them into pieces. Then he gave them to the disciples to give to the people. All of them ate and were satisfied. The disciples picked up 12 baskets of leftover pieces.

One day Jesus was praying alone. Only his disciples were with him. He asked them, "Who do the crowds say I am?"

They replied, "Some say John the Baptist. Others say Elijah. Still others say that one of the prophets of long ago has come back to life."

"But what about you?" he asked. "Who do you say I am?"

Peter answered, "God's Messiah."

Jesus strongly warned them not to tell this to anyone. He said, "The Son of Man must suffer many things. The elders will not accept him. The chief priests and the teachers of the law will not accept him either. He must be killed and on the third day rise from the dead."

Then he said to all of them, "Whoever wants to follow me must say no to themselves. They must pick up their cross every day and follow me. Whoever wants to save their life will lose it. But whoever loses their life for me will save it. What good is it if someone gains the whole world but loses or gives up their very self? Suppose someone is ashamed of me and my words. The Son of Man will come in his glory and in the glory of the Father and the holy angels. Then he will be ashamed of that person.

"What I'm about to tell you is true. Some who are standing here will not die before they see God's kingdom."

About eight days after Jesus said this, he went up on a mountain to pray. He took Peter, John and James with him. As he was praying, the appearance of his face changed. His clothes became as bright as a flash

of lightning. Two men, Moses and Elijah, appeared in shining glory. Jesus and the two of them talked together. They talked about how he would be leaving them soon. This was going to happen in Jerusalem. Peter and his companions had been very sleepy. But then they became completely awake. They saw Jesus' glory and the two men standing with him. As the men were leaving Jesus, Peter spoke up. "Master," he said to him, "it is good for us to be here. Let us put up three shelters. One will be for you, one for Moses, and one for Elijah." Peter didn't really know what he was saying.

While he was speaking, a cloud appeared and covered them. The disciples were afraid as they entered the cloud. A voice came from the cloud. It said, "This is my Son, and I have chosen him. Listen to him." When the voice had spoken, they found that Jesus was alone. The disciples kept quiet about this. They didn't tell anyone at that time what they had seen.

The next day Jesus and those who were with him came down from the mountain. A large crowd met Jesus. A man in the crowd called out. "Teacher," he said, "I beg you to look at my son. He is my only child. A spirit takes hold of him, and he suddenly screams. It throws him into fits so that he foams at the mouth. It hardly ever leaves him. It is destroying him. I begged your disciples to drive it out. But they couldn't do it."

"You unbelieving and evil people!" Jesus replied. "How long do I have to stay with you? How long do

I have to put up with you?" Then he said to the man, "Bring your son here."

Even while the boy was coming, the demon threw him into a fit. The boy fell to the ground. But Jesus ordered the evil spirit to leave the boy. Then Jesus healed him and gave him back to his father. They were all amazed at God's greatness.

Everyone was wondering about all that Jesus did. Then Jesus said to his disciples, "Listen carefully to what I am about to tell you. The Son of Man is going to be handed over to men." But they didn't understand what this meant. That was because it was hidden from them. And they were afraid to ask Jesus about it.

The disciples began to argue about which one of them would be the most important person. Jesus knew what they were thinking. So he took a little child and stood the child beside him. Then he spoke to them. "Anyone who welcomes this little child in my name welcomes me," he said. "And anyone who welcomes me welcomes the one who sent me. The one considered least important among all of you is really the most important."

"Master," said John, "we saw someone driving out demons in your name. We tried to stop him, because he is not one of us."

"Do not stop him," Jesus said. "Anyone who is not against you is for you."

♔ Three ♔

The time grew near for Jesus to be taken up to heaven. So he made up his mind to go to Jerusalem. He sent messengers on ahead. They went into a Samaritan village to get things ready for him. But the people there did not welcome Jesus. That was because he was heading for Jerusalem. The disciples James and John saw this. They asked, "Lord, do you want us to call down fire from heaven to destroy them?" But Jesus turned and commanded them not to do it. Then Jesus and his disciples went on to another village.

Once Jesus and those who were with him were walking along the road. A man said to Jesus, "I will follow you no matter where you go."

Jesus replied, "Foxes have dens. Birds have nests. But the Son of Man has no place to lay his head."

He said to another man, "Follow me."

But the man replied, "Lord, first let me go and bury my father."

Jesus said to him, "Let dead people bury their own dead. You go and tell others about God's kingdom."

Still another person said, "I will follow you, Lord. But first let me go back and say goodbye to my family."

Jesus replied, "Suppose someone starts to plough and then looks back. That person is not fit for service in God's kingdom."

After this the Lord appointed 72 others. He sent them

out two by two ahead of him. They went to every town and place where he was about to go. He told them, "The harvest is huge, but the workers are few. So ask the Lord of the harvest to send out workers into his harvest field. Go! I am sending you out like lambs among wolves. Do not take a purse or bag or sandals. And don't greet anyone on the road.

"When you enter a house, first say, 'May this house be blessed with peace.' If someone there works to bring peace, your blessing of peace will rest on them. If not, it will return to you. Stay there, and eat and drink anything they give you. Workers are worthy of their pay. Do not move around from house to house.

"When you enter a town and are welcomed, eat what is given to you. Heal the ill people who are there. Tell them, 'God's kingdom has come near to you.' But what if you enter a town and are not welcomed? Then go into its streets and say, 'We wipe from our feet even the dust of your town. We do it to warn you. But here is what you can be sure of. God's kingdom has come near.' I tell you this. On judgment day it will be easier for Sodom than for that town.

"How terrible it will be for you, Chorazin! How terrible for you, Bethsaida! Suppose the miracles done in you had been done in Tyre and Sidon. They would have turned away from their sins long ago. They would have put on the rough clothing people wear when they're sad. They would have sat down in ashes. On judgment day it will be easier for Tyre and Sidon than for you. And what about you, Capernaum? Will you be lifted up to the heavens? No! You will go down to the place of the dead.

"Whoever listens to you listens to me. Whoever does not accept you does not accept me. But whoever does not accept me does not accept the one who sent me."

The 72 returned with joy. They said, "Lord, even the demons obey us when we speak in your name."

Jesus replied, "I saw Satan fall like lightning from heaven. I have given you authority to walk all over snakes and scorpions. You will be able to destroy all the power of the enemy. Nothing will harm you. But do not be glad when the evil spirits obey you. Instead, be glad that your names are written in heaven."

At that time Jesus was full of joy through the Holy Spirit. He said, "I praise you, Father. You are Lord of heaven and earth. You have hidden these things from wise and educated people. But you have shown them to little children. Yes, Father. This is what you wanted to do.

"My Father has given all things to me. The Father is the only one who knows who the Son is. And the only

ones who know the Father are the Son and those to whom the Son chooses to make the Father known."

Then Jesus turned to his disciples. He said to them in private, "Blessed are the eyes that see what you see. I tell you, many prophets and kings wanted to see what you see. But they didn't see it. They wanted to hear what you hear. But they didn't hear it."

One day an authority on the law stood up to test Jesus. "Teacher," he asked, "what must I do to receive eternal life?"

"What is written in the Law?" Jesus replied. "How do you understand it?"

He answered, "'Love the Lord your God with all your heart and with all your soul. Love him with all your strength and with all your mind.' *(from the Book of Deuteronomy)* And, 'Love your neighbour as you love yourself.'" *(from the Book of Leviticus)*

"You have answered correctly," Jesus replied. "Do that, and you will live."

But the man wanted to make himself look good. So he asked Jesus, "And who is my neighbour?"

Jesus replied, "A man was going down from Jerusalem to Jericho. Robbers attacked him. They stripped off his clothes and beat him. Then they went away, leaving him almost dead. A priest happened to be going down that same road. When he saw the man, he passed by on the other side. A Levite also came by. When he saw the man, he passed by on the other side too. But a Samaritan came to the place where the man was. When he saw the man, he felt sorry for him. He went to him, poured olive oil and wine on his wounds and bandaged them. Then he put the man on his own donkey. He brought him to an inn and took care of him. The next day he took out two silver coins. He gave them to the owner of the inn. 'Take care of him,' he said. 'When I return, I will pay you back for any extra expense you may have.'

"Which of the three do you think was a neighbour to the man who was attacked by robbers?"

The authority on the law replied, "The one who felt sorry for him."

Jesus told him, "Go and do as he did."

Jesus and his disciples went on their way. Jesus came to a village where a woman named Martha lived. She welcomed him into her home. She had a sister named Mary. Mary sat at the Lord's feet listening to what he said. But Martha was busy with all the things that had to be done. She came to Jesus and said, "Lord, my sister has left me to do the work by myself. Don't you care? Tell her to help me!"

"Martha, Martha," the Lord answered. "You are worried and upset about many things. But few things are needed. Really, only one thing is needed. Mary has chosen what is better. And it will not be taken away from her."

One day Jesus was praying in a certain place. When he finished, one of his disciples spoke to him. "Lord,"

66

he said, "teach us to pray, just as John taught his disciples."

Jesus said to them, "When you pray, this is what you should say.

"'Father,
may your name be honoured.
May your kingdom come.
Give us each day our daily bread.
Forgive us our sins,
  as we also forgive everyone who sins
      against us.
Keep us from falling into sin when we are
      tempted.'"

Then Jesus said to them, "Suppose you have a friend. You go to him at midnight and say, 'Friend, lend me three loaves of bread. A friend of mine on a journey has come to stay with me. I have no food to give him.' And suppose the one inside answers, 'Don't bother me. The door is already locked. My children and I are in bed. I can't get up and give you anything.' I tell you, that person will not get up. And he won't give you bread just because he is your friend. But because you keep bothering him, he will surely get up. He will give you as much as you need.

"So here is what I say to you. Ask, and it will be given to you. Search, and you will find. Knock, and the door will be opened to you. Everyone who asks will receive. The one who searches will find. And the door will be opened to the one who knocks.

"Fathers, suppose your son asks for a fish. Which of you will give him a snake instead? Or suppose he asks for an egg. Which of you will give him a scorpion? Even though you are evil, you know how to give good gifts to your children. How much more will your Father who is in heaven give the Holy Spirit to those who ask him!"

Jesus was driving out a demon. The man who had the demon could not speak. When the demon left, the man began to speak. The crowd was amazed. But some of them said, "Jesus is driving out demons by the power of Beelzebul, the prince of demons." Others tested Jesus by asking for a sign from heaven.

Jesus knew what they were thinking. So he said to them, "Any kingdom that fights against itself will be destroyed. A family that is divided against itself will fall. If Satan fights against himself, how can his kingdom stand? I say this because of what you claim. You say I drive out demons by the power of Beelzebul. Suppose I do drive out demons with Beelzebul's help. With whose help do your followers drive them out? So then, they will be your judges. But suppose I drive out demons with the help of God's powerful finger. Then God's kingdom has come upon you.

"When a strong man is completely armed and

guards his house, what he owns is safe. But when someone stronger attacks, he is overpowered. The attacker takes away the armour the man had trusted in. Then he divides up what he has stolen.

"Whoever is not with me is against me. And whoever does not gather with me scatters.

"What happens when an evil spirit comes out of a person? It goes through dry areas looking for a place to rest. But it doesn't find it. Then it says, 'I will return to the house I left.' When it arrives there, it finds the house swept clean and put in order. Then the evil spirit goes and takes seven other spirits more evil than itself. They go in and live there. That person is worse off than before."

As Jesus was saying these things, a woman in the crowd called out. She shouted, "Blessed is the mother who gave you birth and fed you."

He replied, "Instead, blessed are those who hear God's word and obey it."

As the crowds grew larger, Jesus spoke to them. "The people of today are evil," he said. "They ask for a sign from God. But none will be given except the sign of Jonah. He was a sign from God to the people of Nineveh. In the same way, the Son of Man will be a sign from God to the people of today. The Queen of the South will stand up on judgment day with the people now living. And she will prove that they are guilty. She came from very far away to listen to Solomon's wisdom. And now something more important than

Solomon is here. The men of Nineveh will stand up on judgment day with the people now living. And the Ninevites will prove that those people are guilty. The men of Nineveh turned away from their sins when Jonah preached to them. And now something more important than Jonah is here.

"No-one lights a lamp and hides it. No-one puts it under a bowl. Instead, they put a lamp on its stand. Then those who come in can see the light. Your eye is like a lamp for your body. Suppose your eyes are healthy. Then your whole body also is full of light. But suppose your eyes can't see well. Then your body also is full of darkness. So make sure that the light inside you is not darkness. Suppose your whole body is full of light. And suppose no part of it is dark. Then your body will be full of light. It will be just as when a lamp shines its light on you."

Jesus finished speaking. Then a Pharisee invited him to eat with him. So Jesus went in and took his place at the table. But the Pharisee was surprised. He noticed that Jesus did not wash before the meal.

Then the Lord spoke to him. "You Pharisees clean the outside of the cup and dish," he said. "But inside you are full of greed and evil. You foolish people! Didn't the one who made the outside make the inside also? Give freely to poor people to show what is inside you. Then

everything will be clean for you. "How terrible it will be for you Pharisees! You give God a tenth of your garden plants, such as mint and rue. But you have forgotten to be fair and to love God. You should have practised the last things without failing to do the first.

"How terrible for you Pharisees! You love the most important seats in the synagogues. You love having people greet you with respect in the market.

"How terrible for you! You are like graves that are not marked. People walk over them without knowing it."

An authority on the law spoke to Jesus. He said, "Teacher, when you say things like that, you say bad things about us too."

Jesus replied, "How terrible for you authorities on the law! You put such heavy loads on people that they can hardly carry them. But you yourselves will not lift one finger to help them.

"How terrible for you! You build tombs for the prophets. It was your people of long ago who killed them. So you show that you agree with what your people did long ago. They killed the prophets, and now you build the prophets' tombs. So God in his wisdom said, 'I will send prophets and apostles to them. They will kill some. And they will try to hurt others.' So the people of today will be punished. They will pay for all the prophets' blood spilled since the world began. I mean from the blood of Abel to the blood of Zechariah. He was killed between the altar and the temple. Yes, I tell you, the people of today will be punished for all these things.

"How terrible for you authorities on the law! You have taken away the key to the door of knowledge. You yourselves have not entered. And you have stood in the way of those who were entering."

When Jesus went outside, the Pharisees and the teachers of the law strongly opposed him. They threw a lot of questions at him. They set traps for him. They wanted to catch him in something he might say.

During that time a crowd of many thousands had gathered. There were so many people that they were stepping on one another. Jesus spoke first to his disciples. "Be on your guard against the yeast of the Pharisees," he said. "They just pretend to be godly. Everything that is secret will be brought out into the open. Everything that is hidden will be uncovered. What you have said in the dark will be heard in the daylight. What you have whispered to someone behind closed doors will be shouted from the rooftops.

"My friends, listen to me. Don't be afraid of those who kill the body but can't do any more than that. I will show you whom you should be afraid of. Be afraid of the one who has the authority to throw you into hell after you have been killed. Yes, I tell you, be afraid of him. Aren't five sparrows sold for two pennies? But God does not forget even one of them. In fact, he even counts every hair on your head! So don't be afraid. You are worth more than many sparrows.

"What about someone who says in front of others that he knows me? I tell you, the Son of Man will say in front of God's angels that he knows that person. But what about someone who says in front of others that he doesn't know me? I, the Son of Man, will say in front of God's angels that I don't know him. Everyone who speaks a word against the Son of Man will be forgiven. But anyone who speaks evil things against the Holy Spirit will not be forgiven.

"You will be brought before synagogues, rulers and authorities. But do not worry about how to stand up for yourselves or what to say. The Holy Spirit will teach you at that time what you should say."

Someone in the crowd spoke to Jesus. "Teacher," he said, "tell my brother to divide the family property with me."

Jesus replied, "Friend, who made me a judge or umpire between you?" Then he said to them, "Watch out! Be on your guard against wanting to have more and more things. Life is not made up of how much a person has."

Then Jesus told them a story. He said, "A certain rich man's land produced a very large crop. He thought to himself, 'What should I do? I don't have any place to store my crops.'

"Then he said, 'This is what I'll do. I will tear down my barns and build bigger ones. I will store my extra corn in them. I'll say to myself, "You have plenty of corn stored away for many years. Take life easy. Eat, drink and have a good time."'

"But God said to him, 'You foolish man! Tonight I will take your life away from you. Then who will get what you have prepared for yourself?'

"That is how it will be for whoever stores things away for themselves but is not rich in the sight of God."

Then Jesus spoke to his disciples. He said, "I tell you, do not worry. Don't worry about your life and what you will eat. And don't worry about your body and what you will wear. There is more to life than eating. There are more important things for the body than clothes. Think about the ravens. They don't plant or gather crops. They don't have any barns at all. But God feeds them. You are worth much more than birds! Can you add even one hour to your life by worrying? You can't do that very little thing. So why worry about the rest?

"Think about how the wild flowers grow. They don't work or make clothing. But here is what I tell you. Not even Solomon in his royal robes was dressed like one of those flowers. If that is how God dresses the wild grass, how much better will he dress you! After all, the grass is here only today. Tomorrow it is thrown into the fire. Your faith is so small! Don't spend time thinking about what you will eat or drink. Don't worry about it. People who are ungodly run after all those things. Your Father knows that you need them. But put God's kingdom first. Then those other things will also be given to you.

"Little flock, do not be afraid. Your Father has been pleased to give you the kingdom. Sell what you own. Give to those who are poor. Provide purses for yourselves that will not wear out. Store up riches in heaven that will never be used up. There, no thief can come near it. There, no moth can destroy it. Your heart will be where your riches are.

"Be dressed and ready to serve. Keep your lamps burning. Be like servants waiting for their master to return from a wedding dinner. When he comes and

knocks, they can open the door for him at once. It will be good for those servants whose master finds them ready when he comes. What I'm about to tell you is true. The master will then dress himself so he can serve them. He will have them take their places at the table. And he will come and wait on them. It will be good for those servants whose master finds them ready. It will even be good if he comes in the middle of the night or towards morning. But here is what you must understand. Suppose the owner of the house knew at what hour the robber was coming. He would not have let his house be broken into. You also must be ready. The Son of Man will come at an hour when you don't expect him."

Peter asked, "Lord, are you telling this story to us, or to everyone?"

The Lord answered, "Suppose a master puts one of his servants in charge of his other servants. The servant's job is to give them the food they are to receive at the right time. The master wants a faithful and wise manager for this. It will be good for the

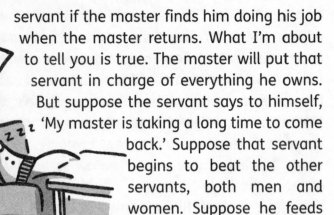

servant if the master finds him doing his job when the master returns. What I'm about to tell you is true. The master will put that servant in charge of everything he owns. But suppose the servant says to himself, 'My master is taking a long time to come back.' Suppose that servant begins to beat the other servants, both men and women. Suppose he feeds himself. And suppose he drinks until he gets drunk. The master of that servant will come back on a day the servant doesn't expect him. The master will return at an hour the servant doesn't know. Then the master will cut him to pieces. He will send the servant to the place where unbelievers go.

"Suppose a servant knows the master's wishes. But the servant doesn't get ready and doesn't do what the master wants. Then that servant will receive a heavy beating. But suppose the servant does not know his master's wishes. And suppose the servant does things for which he should be punished. He will receive a lighter beating. "Much will be required of everyone who has been given much. Even more will be asked of the person who is supposed to take care of much.

"I have come to bring fire on the earth. How I wish the fire had already started! But I have a baptism of suffering to go through. And I must go through it. Do you think I came to bring peace on earth? No, I tell you. I have come to separate people. From now on there will be five members in a family, each one against the other. There will be three against two and two against three. They will be separated. Father will turn against son and son against father. Mother will turn against daughter and daughter against mother. Mother-in-law will turn against daughter-in-law and daughter-in-law against mother-in-law."

Jesus spoke to the crowd. He said, "You see a cloud rising in the west. Right away you say, 'It's going to rain.' And it does. The south wind blows. So you say, 'It's going to be hot.' And it is. You pretenders! You know how to understand the appearance of the earth and the sky. Why can't you understand the meaning of what is happening right now?

"Why don't you judge for yourselves what is right? Suppose someone has a claim against you, and you are on your way to court. Try hard to settle the matter on the way. If you don't, that person may drag you off to the judge. The judge may turn you over to the officer. And the officer may throw you into prison. I tell you, you will not get out until you have paid the very last penny!"

Some people who were there at that time told Jesus about certain Galileans. Pilate had mixed their blood with their sacrifices. Jesus said, "These people from Galilee suffered greatly. Do you think they were worse sinners than all the other Galileans? I tell you, no! But unless you turn away from your sins, you will all die too. Or what about the 18 people in Siloam? They died when the tower fell on them. Do you think they were more guilty than all the others living in Jerusalem? I tell you, no! But unless you turn away from your sins, you will all die too."

Then Jesus told a story. "A man had a fig tree," he said. "It was growing in his vineyard. When he went to look for fruit on it, he didn't find any. So he went to the man who took care of the vineyard. He said, 'For three years now I've been coming to look for fruit on this fig tree. But I haven't found any. Cut it down! Why should it use up the soil?'

"'Sir,' the man replied, 'leave it alone for one more year. I'll dig around it and feed it. If it bears fruit next year, fine! If not, then cut it down.'"

Jesus was teaching in one of the synagogues on a Sabbath day. A woman there had been disabled by an evil spirit for 18 years. She was bent over and could not stand up straight. Jesus saw her. He asked her to come to him. He said to her, "Woman, you will no longer be disabled. I am about to set you free." Then he put his hands on her. Right away she stood up straight and praised God.

Jesus had healed the woman on the Sabbath day. This made the synagogue leader angry. He told the people, "There are six days for work. So come and be healed on those days. But do not come on the Sabbath day."

The Lord answered him, "You pretenders! Doesn't

each of you go to the barn and untie your ox or donkey on the Sabbath day? Then don't you lead it out to give it water? This woman is a member of Abraham's family line. But Satan has kept her disabled for 18 long years. Shouldn't she be set free on the Sabbath day from what was keeping her disabled?"

When Jesus said this, all those who opposed him were put to shame. But the people were delighted. They loved all the wonderful things he was doing.

Then Jesus asked, "What is God's kingdom like? What can I compare it to? It is like a mustard seed. Someone took the seed and planted it in a garden. It grew and became a tree. The birds sat in its branches."

Again he asked, "What can I compare God's kingdom to? It is like yeast that a woman used. She mixed it into 60 pounds of flour. The yeast worked its way all through the dough."

Then Jesus went through the towns and villages, teaching the people. He was on his way to Jerusalem. Someone asked him, "Lord, are only a few people going to be saved?"

He said to them, "Try very hard to enter through the narrow door. I tell you, many will try to enter and will not be able to. The owner of the house will get up and close the door. Then you will stand outside knocking and begging. You will say, 'Sir, open the door for us.'

"But he will answer, 'I don't know you. And I don't know where you come from.'

"Then you will say, 'We ate and drank with you. You taught in our streets.'

"But he will reply, 'I don't know you. And I don't know where you come from. Get away from me, all you who do evil!'

"You will weep and grind your teeth together when you see those who are in God's kingdom. You will see Abraham, Isaac and Jacob and all the prophets there. But you yourselves will be thrown out. People will come from east and west and north and south. They will take their places at the feast in God's kingdom. Then the last will be first. And the first will be last."

At that time some Pharisees came to Jesus. They said to him, "Leave this place. Go somewhere else. Herod wants to kill you."

He replied, "Go and tell that fox, 'I will keep on driving out demons. I will keep on healing people today and tomorrow. And on the third day I will reach my goal.' In any case, I must keep going today and tomorrow and the next day. Certainly no prophet can die outside Jerusalem!

"Jerusalem! Jerusalem! You kill the prophets and throw stones in order to kill those who are sent to you. Many times I have wanted to gather your people together. I have wanted to be like a hen who gathers her chicks under her wings. And you would not let me. Look, your house is left empty. I tell you, you will not see me again until you say, 'Blessed is the one who comes in the name of the Lord.'" *(from Psalm 118)*

One Sabbath day, Jesus went to eat in the house of a well-known Pharisee. While he was there, he was being carefully watched. In front of him was a man whose body was badly swollen. Jesus turned to the Pharisees and the authorities on the law. He asked them, "Is it breaking the Law to heal on the Sabbath day?" But they remained silent. So Jesus took hold of the man and healed him. Then he sent him away.

He asked them another question. He said, "Suppose one of you has a child or an ox that falls into a well on the Sabbath day. Wouldn't you pull it out right away?" And they had nothing to say.

Jesus noticed how the guests picked the places of honour at the table. So he told them a story. He said, "Suppose someone invites you to a wedding feast. Do not take the place of honour. A person more important than you may have been invited. If so, the host who invited both of you will come to you. He will say, 'Give this person your seat.' Then you will be filled with shame. You will have to take the least important place. But when you are invited, take the lowest place. Then your host will come over to you. He will say, 'Friend, move up to a better place.' Then you will be honoured in front of all the other guests. All those who lift themselves up will be made humble. And those who make themselves humble will be lifted up."

Then Jesus spoke to his host. "Suppose you give a lunch or a dinner," he said. "Do not invite your friends, your brothers or sisters, or your relatives, or your rich neighbours. If you do, they may invite you to eat with them. So you will be paid back. But when you give a banquet, invite those who are poor. Also invite those who can't see or walk. Then you will be blessed. Your guests can't pay you back. But you will be paid back when those who are right with God rise from the dead."

One of the people at the table with Jesus heard him say those things. So he said to Jesus, "Blessed is the one who will eat at the feast in God's kingdom."

Jesus replied, "A certain man was preparing a great banquet. He invited many guests. Then the day of the banquet arrived. He sent his servant to those who had been invited. The servant told them, 'Come. Everything is ready now.'

"But they all had the same idea. They began to make excuses. The first one said, 'I have just bought a field. I have to go and see it. Please excuse me.'

"Another said, 'I have just bought five pairs of oxen. I'm on my way to try them out. Please excuse me.'

"Still another said, 'I just got married, so I can't come.'

"The servant came back and reported this to his

master. "Then the owner of the house became angry. He ordered his servant, 'Go out quickly into the streets and lanes of the town. Bring in those who are poor. Also bring those who can't see or walk.'

"'Sir,' the servant said, 'what you ordered has been done. But there is still room.'

"Then the master told his servant, 'Go out to the roads. Go out to the country lanes. Make the people come in. I want my house to be full. I tell you, not one of those people who were invited will get a taste of my banquet.'"

Large crowds were travelling with Jesus. He turned and spoke to them. He said, "Anyone who comes to me must hate their father and mother. They must hate their wife and children. They must hate their brothers and sisters. And they must hate even their own life. Unless they do this, they can't be my disciple. Whoever doesn't carry their cross and follow me can't be my disciple.

"Suppose one of you wants to build a tower. Won't you sit down first and figure out how much it will cost? Then you will see whether you have enough money to finish it. Suppose you start building and are not able to finish. Then everyone who sees what you have done will laugh at you. They will say, 'This person started to build but wasn't able to finish.'

"Or suppose a king is about to go to war against another king. And suppose he has 10,000 men, while the other has 20,000 coming against him. Won't he first sit down and think about whether he can win? And suppose he decides he can't win. Then he will send some men to ask how peace can be made. He will do this while the other king is still far away. In the same way, you must give up everything you have. Those of you who don't cannot be my disciple.

"Salt is good. But suppose it loses its saltiness. How can it be made salty again? It is not good for the soil. And it is not good for the trash pile. It will be thrown out.

"Whoever has ears should listen."

The tax collectors and sinners were all gathering around to hear Jesus. But the Pharisees and the teachers of the law were whispering among themselves. They said, "This man welcomes sinners and eats with them."

Then Jesus told them a story. He said, "Suppose one of you has 100 sheep and loses one of them. Won't he leave the 99 in the open country? Won't he go and look for the one lost sheep until he finds it? When he finds it, he will joyfully put it on his shoulders and go home. Then he will call his friends and neighbours together. He will say, 'Be joyful with me. I have found my lost sheep.' I tell you, it will be the same in heaven. There will be great joy when one sinner turns away from sin. Yes, there will be more joy than for 99 godly people who do not need to turn away from their sins.

"Or suppose a woman has ten silver coins and loses one. Won't she light a lamp and sweep the house? Won't she search carefully until she finds the coin?

And when she finds it, she will call her friends and neighbours together. She will say, 'Be joyful with me. I have found my lost coin.' I tell you, it is the same in heaven. There is joy in heaven over one sinner who turns away from sin."

Jesus continued, "There was a man who had two sons. The younger son spoke to his father. He said, 'Father, give me my share of the family property.' So the father divided his property between his two sons.

"Not long after that, the younger son packed up all he had. Then he left for a country far away. There he wasted his money on wild living. He spent everything he had. "Then the whole country ran low on food. So the son didn't have what he needed. He went to work for someone who lived in that country. That person sent the son to the fields to feed the pigs. The son wanted to fill his stomach with the food the pigs were eating. But no-one gave him anything.

"Then he began to think clearly again. He said, 'How many of my father's hired servants have more than enough food! But here I am dying from hunger! I will get up and go back to my father. I will say to him, "Father, I have sinned against heaven. And I have sinned against you. I am no longer fit to be called your son. Make me like one of your hired servants."' So he got up and went to his father.

"While the son was still a long way off, his father saw him. He was filled with tender love for his son. He ran to him. He threw his arms around him and kissed him.

"The son said to him, 'Father, I have sinned against

heaven and against you. I am no longer fit to be called your son.'

"But the father said to his servants, 'Quick! Bring the best robe and put it on him. Put a ring on his finger and sandals on his feet. Bring the fattest calf and kill it. Let's have a feast and celebrate. This son of mine was dead. And now he is alive again. He was lost. And now he is found.' So they began to celebrate.

"The elder son was in the field. When he came near the house, he heard music and dancing. So he called one of the servants. He asked him what was going on. 'Your brother has come home,' the servant replied. 'Your father has killed the fattest calf. He has done this because your brother is back safe and sound.'

"The older brother became angry. He refused to go in. So his father went out and begged him. But he answered his father, 'Look! All these years I've worked like a slave for you. I have always obeyed your orders. You never gave me even a young goat so I could celebrate with my friends. But this son of yours wasted your money with some prostitutes. Now he comes home. And for him you kill the fattest calf!'

"'My son,' the father said, 'you are always with me. Everything I have is yours. But we had to celebrate and be glad. This brother of yours was dead. And now he is alive again. He was lost. And now he is found.'"

Jesus told his disciples another story. He said, "There was a rich man who had a manager. Some said that the manager was wasting what the rich man owned.

So the rich man told him to come in. He asked him, 'What is this I hear about you? Tell me exactly how you have handled what I own. You can't be my manager any longer.'

"The manager said to himself, 'What will I do now? My master is taking away my job. I'm not strong enough to dig. And I'm too ashamed to beg. I know what I'm going to do. I'll do something so that when I lose my job here, people will welcome me into their houses.'

"So he called in each person who owed his master something. He asked the first one, 'How much do you owe my master?'

"'I owe 900 gallons of olive oil,' he replied.

"The manager told him, 'Take your bill. Sit down quickly and change it to 450 gallons.'

"Then he asked the second one, 'And how much do you owe?'

"'I owe 1,000 bushels of wheat,' he replied.

"The manager told him, 'Take your bill and change it to 800 bushels.'

"The manager had not been honest. But the

master praised him for being clever. The people of this world are clever in dealing with those who are like themselves. They are more clever than God's people. I tell you, use the riches of this world to help others. In that way, you will make friends for yourselves. Then when your riches are gone, you will be welcomed into your eternal home in heaven.

"Suppose you can be trusted with very little. Then you can be trusted with a lot. But suppose you are not honest with very little. Then you will not be honest with a lot. Suppose you have not been worthy of trust in handling worldly wealth. Then who will trust you with true riches? Suppose you have not been worthy of trust in handling someone else's property. Then who will give you property of your own?

"No-one can serve two masters at the same time. Either you will hate one of them and love the other. Or you will be faithful to one and dislike the other. You can't serve God and money at the same time."

The Pharisees loved money. They heard all that Jesus said and made fun of him. Jesus said to them, "You try to make yourselves look good in the eyes of other people. But God knows your hearts. What people think is worth a lot is hated by God.

"The teachings of the Law and the Prophets were preached until John the Baptist came. Since then, the good news of God's kingdom is being preached. And everyone is trying very hard to enter it. It is easier for heaven and earth to disappear than for the smallest part of a letter to drop out of the Law.

"Anyone who divorces his wife and marries another woman commits adultery. Also, the man who marries a divorced woman commits adultery.

"Once there was a rich man. He was dressed in purple cloth and fine linen. He lived an easy life every day. A man named Lazarus was placed at his gate. Lazarus was a beggar. His body was covered with sores. Even dogs came and licked his sores. All he wanted was to eat what fell from the rich man's table.

"The time came when the beggar died. The angels carried him to Abraham's side. The rich man also died and was buried. In the place of the dead, the rich man was suffering terribly. He looked up and saw Abraham far away. Lazarus was by his side. So the rich man called out, 'Father Abraham! Have pity on me! Send Lazarus to dip the tip of his finger in water. Then he can cool my tongue with it. I am in terrible pain in this fire.'

"But Abraham replied, 'Son, remember what happened in your lifetime. You received your good things. Lazarus received bad things. Now he is comforted here, and you are in terrible pain. Besides, a wide space has been placed between us and you. So those who want to go from here to you can't go. And no-one can cross over from there to us.'

"The rich man answered, 'Then I beg you, father Abraham. Send Lazarus to my family. I have five brothers. Let Lazarus warn them. Then they will not come to this place of terrible suffering.'

"Abraham replied, 'They have the teachings of Moses and the Prophets. Let your brothers listen to them.'

"'No, father Abraham,' he said. 'But if someone from the dead goes to them, they will turn away from their sins.'

"Abraham said to him, 'They do not listen to Moses and the Prophets. So they will not be convinced even if someone rises from the dead.'"

Jesus spoke to his disciples. "Things that make people sin are sure to come," he said. "But how terrible it will be for anyone who causes those things to come! Suppose people lead one of these little ones to sin. It would be better for those people to be thrown into the sea with a millstone tied around their neck. So watch what you do.

"If your brother or sister sins against you, tell them they are wrong. Then if they turn away from their sins, forgive them. Suppose they sin against you seven times in one day. And suppose they come back to you each time and say, 'I'm sorry.' You must forgive them."

The apostles said to the Lord, "Give us more faith!"

He replied, "Suppose you have faith as small as a mustard seed. Then you can say to this mulberry tree, 'Be pulled up. Be planted in the sea.' And it will obey you.

"Suppose one of you has a servant ploughing or looking after the sheep. And suppose the servant came in from the field. Will you say to him, 'Come along now and sit down to eat'? No. Instead, you will say, 'Prepare my supper. Get yourself ready. Wait on me while I eat and drink. Then after that you can eat and drink.' Will you thank the servant because he did what he was told to do? It's the same with you. Suppose you have done everything you were told to do. Then you should say, 'We are not worthy to serve you. We have only done our duty.'"

Jesus was on his way to Jerusalem. He travelled along the border between Samaria and Galilee. As he was going into a village, ten men met him. They had a skin disease. They were standing close by. And they called out in a loud voice, "Jesus! Master! Have pity on us!"

Jesus saw them and said, "Go. Show yourselves to the priests." While they were on the way, they were healed.

When one of them saw that he was healed, he
came back. He praised God in a loud voice.
He threw himself at Jesus' feet and thanked
him. The man was a Samaritan.

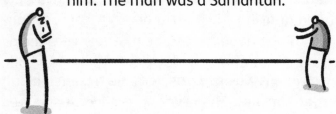

Jesus asked, "Weren't all ten healed?
Where are the other nine? Didn't anyone
else return and give praise to God except
this outsider?" Then Jesus said to
him, "Get up and go. Your faith has
healed you."

Once the Pharisees asked Jesus when God's kingdom
would come. He replied, "The coming of God's kingdom
is not something you can see. People will not say, 'Here
it is.' Or, 'There it is.' That's because God's kingdom is
among you."

Then Jesus spoke to his disciples. "The time is
coming," he said, "when you will long to see one of the
days of the Son of Man. But you won't see it. People will
tell you, 'There he is!' Or, 'Here he is!' Don't go running
off after them. When the Son of Man comes, he will
be like the lightning. It flashes and lights up the sky
from one end to the other. But first the Son of Man

must suffer many things. He will not be accepted by the people of today.

"Remember how it was in the days of Noah. It will be the same when the Son of Man comes. People were eating and drinking. They were getting married. They were giving their daughters to be married. They did all those things right up to the day Noah entered the ark. Then the flood came and destroyed them all.

"It was the same in the days of Lot. People were eating and drinking. They were buying and selling. They were planting and building. But on the day Lot left Sodom, fire and sulphur rained down from heaven. And all the people were destroyed.

"It will be just like that on the day the Son of Man is shown to the world. Suppose someone is on the housetop on that day. And suppose what they own is inside the house. They should not go down to get what they own. No-one in the field should go back for anything either. Remember Lot's wife! Whoever tries to keep their life will lose it. Whoever loses their life will keep it. I tell you, on that night two people will be in one bed. One person will be taken and the other left. Two women will be grinding corn together. One will be taken and the other left."

"Where, Lord?" his disciples asked.

He replied, "The vultures will gather where there is a dead body."

Jesus told his disciples a story. He wanted to show them that they should always pray and not give up.

He said, "In a certain town there was a judge. He didn't have any respect for God or care about what people thought. A widow lived in that town. She came to the judge again and again. She kept begging him, 'Make things right for me. Someone is treating me badly.'

"For some time the judge refused. But finally he said to himself, 'I don't have any respect for God. I don't care about what people think. But this widow keeps bothering me. So I will see that things are made right for her. If I don't, she will someday come and attack me!'"

The Lord said, "Listen to what the unfair judge says. God's chosen people cry out to him day and night. Won't he make things right for them? Will he keep putting them off? I tell you, God will see that things are made right for them. He will make sure it happens quickly. "But when the Son of Man comes, will he find people on earth who have faith?"

Jesus told a story to some people who were sure they were right with God. They looked down on everyone else. He said to them, "Two men went up to the temple to pray. One was a Pharisee. The other was a tax collector. The Pharisee stood by himself and prayed. 'God, I thank you that I am not like other people,' he said. 'I am not like robbers or those who do other evil things. I am not like those who commit adultery. I am not even like this tax collector. I fast twice a week. And I give a tenth of all I get.'

"But the tax collector stood not very far away. He would not even look up to heaven. He brought his hand to his heart and prayed. He said, 'God, have mercy on me. I am a sinner.'

"I tell you, the tax collector went home accepted by God. But not the Pharisee. All those who lift themselves up will be made humble. And those who make themselves humble will be lifted up."

People were also bringing babies to Jesus. They wanted him to place his hands on the babies. When the disciples saw this, they told the people to stop. But Jesus asked the children to come to him. "Let the little children come to me," he said. "Don't keep them away. God's kingdom belongs to people like them. What I'm about to tell you is true. Anyone who will not receive God's kingdom like a little child will never enter it."

A certain ruler asked Jesus a question. "Good teacher," he said, "what must I do to receive eternal life?"

"Why do you call me good?" Jesus answered. "No-one is good except God. You know what the commandments say. 'Do not commit adultery. Do not commit murder. Do not steal. Do not be a false witness. Honour your father and mother.'" *(from the Books of Exodus and Deuteronomy)*

"I have obeyed all those commandments since I was a boy," the ruler said.

When Jesus heard this, he said to him, "You are still missing one thing. Sell everything you have. Give the money to those who are poor. You will have treasure in heaven. Then come and follow me."

When the ruler heard this, he became very sad. He was very rich. Jesus looked at him. Then he said, "How hard it is for rich people to enter God's kingdom! Is it hard for a camel to go through the eye of a needle? It is even harder for someone who is rich to enter God's kingdom!"

Those who heard this asked, "Then who can be saved?"

Jesus replied, "Things that are impossible with people are possible with God."

Peter said to him, "We have left everything we had in order to follow you!"

"What I'm about to tell you is true," Jesus said to them. "Has anyone left home or wife or husband or brothers or sisters or parents or children for God's kingdom? They will receive many times as much in this world. In the world to come they will receive eternal life."

Jesus took the 12 disciples to one side. He told them,

"We are going up to Jerusalem. Everything that the prophets wrote about the Son of Man will come true. He will be handed over to the Gentiles. They will make fun of him. They will laugh at him and spit on him. They will whip him and kill him. On the third day, he will rise from the dead!"

The disciples did not understand any of this. Its meaning was hidden from them. So they didn't know what Jesus was talking about.

Jesus was approaching Jericho. A blind man was sitting by the side of the road begging. The blind man heard the crowd going by. He asked what was happening. They told him, "Jesus of Nazareth is passing by."

So the blind man called out, "Jesus! Son of David! Have mercy on me!"

Those who led the way commanded him to stop. They told him to be quiet. But he shouted even louder, "Son of David! Have mercy on me!"

Jesus stopped and ordered the man to be brought to him. When the man came near, Jesus spoke to him. "What do you want me to do for you?" Jesus asked.

"Lord, I want to be able to see," the blind man replied.

Jesus said to him, "Receive your sight. Your faith has healed you." Right away he could see. He followed Jesus, praising God. When all the people saw it, they also praised God.

Jesus entered Jericho and was passing through. A

man named Zacchaeus lived there. He was a chief tax
collector and was very rich. Zacchaeus wanted to see
who Jesus was. But he was a short man. He could not
see Jesus because of the crowd. So he ran ahead and
climbed a sycamore fig tree. He wanted to see Jesus,
who was coming that way.

Jesus reached the spot where Zacchaeus was. He
looked up and said, "Zacchaeus, come down at once.
I must stay at your house today." So Zacchaeus came
down at once and welcomed him gladly.

All the people saw this. They began to whisper
among themselves. They said, "Jesus has gone to be
the guest of a sinner."

But Zacchaeus stood up. He said, "Look, Lord! Here

and now I give half of what I own to those who are poor. And if I have cheated anybody out of anything, I will pay it back. I will pay back four times the amount I took."

Jesus said to Zacchaeus, "Today salvation has come to your house. You are a member of Abraham's family line. The Son of Man came to look for the lost and save them."

While the people were listening to these things, Jesus told them a story. He was near Jerusalem. The people thought that God's kingdom was going to appear right away. Jesus said, "A man from an important family went to a country far away. He went there to be made king and then return home. So he sent for ten of his slaves. He gave them each about three months' pay. 'Put this money to work until I come back,' he said.

"But those he ruled over hated him. They sent some messengers after him. They were sent to say, 'We don't want this man to be our king.'

"But he was made king and returned home. Then he sent for the slaves he had given the money to. He wanted to find out what they had earned with it.

"The first one came to him. He said, 'Sir, your money has earned ten times as much.'

"'You have done well, my good slave!' his master replied. 'You have been faithful in a very small matter. So I will put you in charge of ten towns.'

"The second slave came to his master. He said, 'Sir, your money has earned five times as much.'

"His master answered, 'I will put you in charge of five towns.'

"Then another slave came. He said, 'Sir, here is your money. I have kept it hidden in a piece of cloth. I was afraid of you. You are a hard man. You take out what you did not put in. You harvest what you did not plant.'

"His master replied, 'I will judge you by your own words, you evil slave! So you knew that I am a hard man? You knew that I take out what I did not put in? You knew that I harvest what I did not plant? Then why didn't you put my money in the bank? When I came back, I could have collected it with interest.'

"Then he said to those standing by, 'Take his money away from him. Give it to the one who has ten times as much.'

"'Sir,' they said, 'he already has ten times as much!'

"He replied, 'I tell you that everyone who has will be given more. But here is what will happen to anyone who has nothing. Even what they have will be taken away from them. And what about my enemies who did not want me to be king over them? Bring them here! Kill them in front of me!'"

♔ Four ♔

A fter Jesus had said this, he went on ahead. He was going up to Jerusalem. He approached Bethphage and Bethany. The hill there was called the Mount of Olives. Jesus sent out two of his disciples. He said to them, "Go to the village ahead of you. As soon as you get there, you will find a donkey's colt tied up. No-one has ever ridden it. Untie it and bring it here. Someone may ask you, 'Why are you untying it?' If so, say, 'The Lord needs it.'"

Those who were sent ahead went and found the young donkey. It was there just as Jesus had told them. They were untying the colt when its owners came. The owners asked them, "Why are you untying the colt?"

They replied, "The Lord needs it."

Then the disciples brought the colt to Jesus. They threw their coats on the young donkey and put Jesus on it. As he went along, people spread their coats on the road.

Jesus came near the place where the road goes down the Mount of Olives. There the whole crowd of disciples began to praise God with joy. In loud voices they praised him for all the miracles they had seen. They shouted,

> "Blessed is the king who comes in the name of the Lord!" *(from Psalm 118)*

> "May there be peace and glory in the highest heaven!"

19:28–19:38

Some of the Pharisees in the crowd spoke to Jesus. "Teacher," they said, "tell your disciples to stop!"

"I tell you," he replied, "if they keep quiet, the stones will cry out."

He approached Jerusalem. When he saw the city, he began to weep. He said, "I wish you had known today what would bring you peace! But now it is hidden from your eyes. The days will come when your enemies will arrive. They will build a wall of dirt up against your city. They will surround you and close you in on every side. You didn't recognise the time when God came to you. So your enemies will smash you to the ground. They will destroy you and all the people inside your walls. They will not leave one stone on top of another."

Then Jesus entered the temple courtyard. He began to drive out those who were selling there. He told them, "It is written that the Lord said, 'My house will be a house where people can pray.' *(from the prophet Isaiah)* But you have made it a 'den for robbers.'" *(from the prophet Jeremiah)*

Every day Jesus was teaching at the temple. But the chief priests and the teachers of the law were trying to kill him. So were the leaders among the people. But they couldn't find any way to do it. All the people were paying close attention to his words.

One day Jesus was teaching the people in the temple courtyard. He was announcing the good news to them.

The chief priests and the teachers of the law came up to him. The elders came with them. "Tell us by what authority you are doing these things," they all said. "Who gave you this authority?"

Jesus replied, "I will also ask you a question. Tell me, was John's baptism from heaven? Or did it come from people?"

They talked to one another about it. They said, "If we say, 'From heaven', he will ask, 'Why didn't you believe him?' But if we say, 'From people', all the people will throw stones at us and kill us. They believe that John was a prophet."

So they answered Jesus, "We don't know where John's baptism came from."

Jesus said, "Then I won't tell you by what authority I am doing these things either."

Jesus went on to tell the people a story. "A man planted a vineyard," he said. "He rented it out to some farmers.

Then he went away for a long time. At harvest time he sent a slave to the renters. They were supposed to give him some of the fruit of the vineyard. But the renters beat the slave. Then they sent him away with nothing. So the man sent another slave. They beat that one and treated him badly. They also sent him away with nothing. The man sent a third slave. The renters wounded him and threw him out.

"Then the owner of the vineyard said, 'What should I do? I have a son, and I love him. I will send him. Maybe they will respect him.'

"But when the renters saw the son, they talked the matter over. 'This is the one who will receive all the owner's property someday,' they said. 'Let's kill him. Then everything will be ours.' So they threw him out of the vineyard. And they killed him.

"What will the owner of the vineyard do to the renters? He will come and kill them. He will give the vineyard to others."

When the people heard this, they said, "We hope this never happens!"

Jesus looked right at them and said, "Here is something I want you to explain the meaning of. It is written,

> "'The stone the builders didn't accept
>   has become the most important stone of
>   all.'   *(from Psalm 118)*

Everyone who falls on that stone will be broken to pieces. But the stone will crush anyone it falls on."

The teachers of the law and the chief priests looked for a way to arrest Jesus at once. They knew he had told that story against them. But they were afraid of the people.

The religious leaders sent spies to keep a close watch on Jesus. The spies pretended to be sincere. They hoped they could trap Jesus with something he would say. Then they could hand him over to the power and authority of the governor. So the spies questioned Jesus. "Teacher," they said, "we know that you speak and teach what is right. We know you don't favour one person over another. You teach the way of God truthfully. Is it right for us to pay taxes to Caesar or not?"

Jesus saw they were trying to trick him. So he said to them, "Show me a silver coin. Whose picture and words are on it?"

"Caesar's," they replied.

He said to them, "Then give back to Caesar what

belongs to Caesar. And give back to God what belongs to God."

They were not able to trap him with what he had said there in front of all the people. Amazed by his answer, they became silent.

The Sadducees do not believe that people rise from the dead. Some of them came to Jesus with a question. "Teacher," they said, "Moses wrote for us about a man's brother who dies. Suppose the brother leaves a wife but has no children. Then the man must marry the widow. He must provide children to carry on his dead brother's name. There were seven brothers. The first one married a woman. He died without leaving any children. The second one married her. And then the third one married her. One after another, the seven brothers married her. They all died. None left any children. Finally, the woman died too. Now then, when the dead rise, whose wife will she be? All seven brothers were married to her."

Jesus replied, "People in this world get married. And their parents give them to be married. But it will not be like that when the dead rise. Those who are considered worthy to take part in the world to come won't get married. And their parents won't give them to be married. They can't die anymore. They are like the angels. They are God's children. They will be given a new form of life when the dead rise. Remember the story of Moses and the burning bush. Even Moses showed that the dead rise. The Lord said to him, 'I am the God of Abraham. I am the God of Isaac. And I am the God of Jacob.' *(from the Book of Exodus)* **He is not the God of the dead. He is the God of the living. In his eyes, everyone is alive."**

Some of the teachers of the law replied, "You have spoken well, teacher!" And no-one dared to ask him any more questions.

Jesus said to them, "Why do people say that the Messiah is the son of David? David himself says in the Book of Psalms,

> "'The Lord said to my Lord,
>   "Sit at my right hand
> until I put your enemies
>   under your control."'   *(from Psalm 110)*

David calls him 'Lord'. So how can he be David's son?"

All the people were listening. Jesus said to his disciples, "Watch out for the teachers of the law. They like to walk around in long robes. They love to be greeted with respect in the market. They love to have the most important seats in the synagogues. They also love to have the places of honour at banquets. They take over the houses of widows. They say long prayers to show off. God will punish these men very much."

As Jesus looked up, he saw rich people putting their gifts into the temple offering boxes. He also saw a poor widow put in two very small copper coins. "What I'm about to tell you is true," Jesus said. "That poor widow has put in more than all the others. All these other people gave a lot because they are rich. But even though she is poor, she put in everything. She had nothing left to live on."

Some of Jesus' disciples were talking about the temple. They spoke about how it was decorated with beautiful stones and with gifts that honoured God. But Jesus asked, "Do you see all this? The time will come when not one stone will be left on top of another. Every stone will be thrown down."

"Teacher," they asked, "when will these things happen? And what will be the sign that they are about to take place?"

Jesus replied, "Keep watch! Be careful that you are not fooled. Many will come in my name. They will claim, 'I am he!' And they will say, 'The time is near!' Do not follow them. Do not be afraid when you hear about wars and about fighting against rulers. Those things must happen first. But the end will not come right away."

Then Jesus said to them, "Nation will fight against nation. Kingdom will fight against kingdom. In many places there will be powerful earthquakes. People will go hungry. There will be terrible diseases. Things will happen that will make people afraid. There will be great and miraculous signs from heaven.

"But before all this, people will arrest you and treat you badly. They will hand you over to synagogues and put you in prison. You will be brought to kings and governors. All this will happen to you because of my name. And so you will be witnesses about me. But make up your mind not to worry in advance about how to stand up for yourselves. I will give you words of wisdom. None of your enemies will be able to withstand them or prove them wrong. Even your parents, brothers, sisters, relatives and friends will hand you over to the authorities. The authorities will put some of you to death. Everyone will hate you because of me. But not a hair on your head will be harmed. Remain strong in the faith, and you will receive eternal life.

"A time is coming when you will see armies surround Jerusalem. Then you will know that it will soon be destroyed. Those who are in Judea should then escape to the mountains. Those in the city should get out. Those in the country should not enter the city. This is the time when God will punish Jerusalem. Everything will come true, just as it has been written. How awful it will be in those days for pregnant women! How awful for nursing mothers! There will be terrible suffering in the land. There will be great anger against those people. Some will be killed by the sword. Others will be taken as prisoners to all the nations. Jerusalem will be taken over by Gentiles until the times of the Gentiles come to an end.

"There will be signs in the sun, moon and stars. The nations of the earth will be in terrible pain. They will be puzzled by the roaring and tossing of the sea. Terror will make people faint. They will be worried about what is happening in the world. The sun, moon and stars will be shaken from their places. At that time people will see the Son of Man coming in a cloud. He will come with power and great glory. When these things begin to take place, stand up. Hold your head up with joy and hope. The time when you will be set free will be very close."

Jesus told them a story. "Look at the fig tree and all the trees," he said. "When you see leaves appear on the branches, you know that summer is near. In the same way, when you see these things happening, you will know that God's kingdom is near.

"What I'm about to tell you is true. The people living now will certainly not pass away until all these things have happened. Heaven and earth will pass away. But my words will never pass away.

"Be careful. If you aren't, your hearts will be loaded down with wasteful living, drunkenness and the worries of life. Then the day the Son of Man returns will close on you like a trap. It will happen suddenly. That day will come on every person who lives on the whole earth. Always keep watching. Pray that you will be able to escape all that is about to happen. Also, pray that you will not be judged guilty when the Son of Man comes."

Each day Jesus taught at the temple. And each evening he went to spend the night on the hill called the Mount of Olives. All the people came to the temple early in the morning. They wanted to hear Jesus speak.

The Feast of Unleavened Bread, called the Passover, was near. The chief priests and the teachers of the law were looking for a way to get rid of Jesus. They were afraid of the people. Then Satan entered Judas, who was called Iscariot. Judas was one of the 12 disciples.

He went to the chief priests and the officers of the temple guard. He talked with them about how he could hand Jesus over to them. They were delighted and agreed to give him money. Judas accepted their offer. He watched for the right time to hand Jesus over to them. He wanted to do it when no crowd was around.

Then the day of Unleavened Bread came. That was the time the Passover lamb had to be sacrificed. Jesus sent Peter and John on ahead. "Go," he told them. "Prepare for us to eat the Passover meal."

"Where do you want us to prepare for it?" they asked.

Jesus replied, "When you enter the city, a man carrying a jar of water will meet you. Follow him to the house he enters. Then say to the owner of the house, 'The Teacher asks, "Where is the guest room? Where can I eat the Passover meal with my disciples?"' He will show you a large upstairs room with furniture already in it. Prepare for us to eat there."

Peter and John left. They found things just as Jesus had told them. So they prepared the Passover meal.

When the hour came, Jesus and his apostles took their places at the table. He said to them, "I have really looked forward to eating this Passover meal with you. I wanted to do this before I suffer. I tell you, I will not eat the Passover meal again until it is celebrated in God's kingdom."

After Jesus took the cup, he gave thanks. He said, "Take this cup and share it among yourselves. I tell you, I will not drink wine with you again until God's kingdom comes."

Then Jesus took bread. He gave thanks and broke it. He handed it to them and said, "This is my body. It is given for you. Every time you eat it, do this in memory of me."

In the same way, after the supper he took the cup. He said, "This cup is the new covenant in my blood. It is poured out for you. But someone here is going to hand me over to my enemies. His hand is with mine on the table. The Son of Man will go to his death, just as God has already decided. But how terrible it will be for the one who hands him over!" The apostles began to ask one another about this. They wondered which one of them would do it.

They also started to argue. They disagreed about which of them was thought to be the most important person. Jesus said to them, "The kings of the Gentiles hold power over their people. And those who order them around call themselves Protectors. But you must not be like that. Instead, the most important among you should be like the youngest. The one who rules should be like the one who serves. Who is more important? Is it the one at the table, or the one who serves? Isn't it the one who is at the table? But I am among you as one who serves. You have stood by me during my troubles. And I give you a kingdom, just as my Father gave me a kingdom. Then you will eat and drink at my table in my kingdom. And you will sit on thrones, judging the 12 tribes of Israel.

"Simon, Simon! Satan has asked to sift all of you disciples like wheat. But I have prayed for you, Simon. I have prayed that your faith will not fail. When you have turned back, help your brothers to be strong."

But Simon replied, "Lord, I am ready to go with you to prison and to death."

Jesus answered, "I tell you, Peter, you will say three times that you don't know me. And you will do it before the cock crows today."

Then Jesus asked the disciples, "Did you need anything when I sent you without a purse, bag or sandals?"

"Nothing," they answered.

He said to them, "But now if you have a purse, take it. And also take a bag. If you don't have a sword, sell your coat and buy one. It is written, 'He was counted among those who had committed crimes.' *(from the prophet Isaiah)* I tell you that what is written about me must come true. Yes, it is already coming true."

The disciples said, "See, Lord, here are two swords."

"Two swords are enough!" he replied.

Jesus went out as usual to the Mount of Olives. His disciples followed him. When they reached the place, Jesus spoke. "Pray that you won't fall into sin when you are tempted," he said to them. Then he went a short distance away from them. There he got down on his knees and prayed. He said, "Father, if you are willing, take this cup of suffering away from me. But do what you want, not what I want." An angel from heaven appeared to Jesus and gave him strength. Because he was very sad and troubled, he prayed even harder. His sweat was like drops of blood falling to the ground.

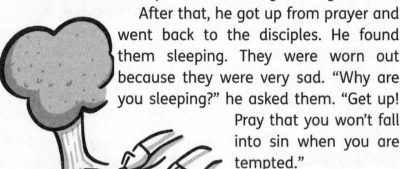

After that, he got up from prayer and went back to the disciples. He found them sleeping. They were worn out because they were very sad. "Why are you sleeping?" he asked them. "Get up! Pray that you won't fall into sin when you are tempted."

While Jesus was still speaking, a crowd came up. The man named Judas was leading them. He was one of the 12 disciples. Judas approached Jesus to kiss him. But Jesus asked him, "Judas, are you handing over the Son of Man with a kiss?"

Jesus' followers saw what was going to happen. So they said, "Lord, should we use our swords against them?" One of them struck the slave of the high priest and cut off his right ear.

But Jesus answered, "Stop this!" And he touched the man's ear and healed him.

Then Jesus spoke to the chief priests, the officers of the temple guard, and the elders. They had all come for him. "Am I leading a band of armed men against you?" he asked. "Do you have to come with swords and clubs? Every day I was with you in the temple courtyard. And you didn't lay a hand on me. But this is your hour. This is when darkness rules."

Then the men arrested Jesus and led him away. They took him into the high priest's house. Peter followed from far away. Some people there started a fire in the middle of the courtyard. Then they sat down together. Peter sat down with them. A female servant saw him sitting there in the firelight. She looked closely at him. Then she said, "This man was with Jesus."

But Peter said he had not been with him. "Woman, I don't know him," he said.

A little later someone else saw Peter. "You also are one of them," he said.

"No," Peter replied. "I'm not!"

About an hour later, another person spoke up. "This fellow must have been with Jesus," he said. "He is from Galilee."

Peter replied, "Man, I don't know what you're talking about!" Just as he was speaking, the cock crowed. The Lord turned and looked right at Peter. Then Peter remembered what the Lord had spoken to him. "The cock will crow today," Jesus had said. "Before it does, you will say three times that you don't know me." Peter went outside. He broke down and cried.

There were men guarding Jesus. They began laughing at him and beating him. They blindfolded him. They said, "Prophesy! Who hit you?" They also said many other things to make fun of him.

At dawn the elders of the people met together. These included the chief priests and the teachers of the law. Jesus was led to them. "If you are the Messiah," they said, "tell us."

Jesus answered, "If I tell you, you will not believe me. And if I asked you, you would not answer. But from now on, the Son of Man will be seated at the right hand of the mighty God."

They all asked, "Are you the Son of God then?"

He replied, "You say that I am."

Then they said, "Why do we need any more witnesses? We have heard it from his own lips."

Then the whole group got up and led Jesus off to Pilate. They began to bring charges against Jesus. They said, "We have found this man misleading our people. He is against paying taxes to Caesar. And he claims to be Messiah, a king."

So Pilate asked Jesus, "Are you the king of the Jews?"

"You have said so," Jesus replied.

Then Pilate spoke to the chief priests and the crowd. He announced, "I find no basis for a charge against this man."

But they kept it up. They said, "His teaching stirs up the people all over Judea. He started in Galilee and has come all the way here."

When Pilate heard this, he asked if the man was from Galilee. He learned that Jesus was from Herod's

area of authority. So Pilate sent Jesus to Herod. At that time Herod was also in Jerusalem.

When Herod saw Jesus, he was very pleased. He had been wanting to see Jesus for a long time. He had heard much about him. He hoped to see Jesus perform a sign of some kind. Herod asked him many questions, but Jesus gave him no answer. The chief priests and the teachers of the law were standing there. With loud shouts they brought charges against him. Herod and his soldiers laughed at him and made fun of him. They dressed him in a beautiful robe. Then they sent him back to Pilate. That day Herod and Pilate became friends. Before this time they had been enemies.

Pilate called together the chief priests, the rulers and the people. He said to them, "You brought me this man. You said he was turning the people against the authorities. I have questioned him in front of you. I have found no basis for your charges against him. Herod hasn't either. So he sent Jesus back to us. As you can see, Jesus has done nothing that is worthy of death. So I will just have him whipped and let him go."

But the whole crowd shouted, "Kill this man! But let Barabbas go!" Barabbas had been thrown into prison. He had taken part in a struggle in the city against the authorities. He had also committed murder.

Pilate wanted to let Jesus go. So he made an appeal to the crowd again. But they kept shouting, "Crucify him! Crucify him!"

Pilate spoke to them for the third time. "Why?" he asked. "What wrong has this man done? I have found no reason to have him put to death. So I will just have him whipped and let him go."

But with loud shouts they kept calling for Jesus to be crucified. The people's shouts won out. So Pilate decided to give them what they wanted. He set free the man they asked for. The man had been thrown in prison for murder and for fighting against the authorities. Pilate handed Jesus over to them so they could carry out their plans.

As the soldiers led Jesus away, they took hold of Simon. Simon was from Cyrene. He was on his way in from the country. They put a wooden cross on his shoulders. Then they made him carry it behind Jesus. A large number of people followed Jesus. Some were women whose hearts were filled with sorrow. They cried loudly because of him. Jesus turned and said to them, "Daughters of Jerusalem, do not weep for me. Weep for yourselves and for your children. The time will come when you will say, 'Blessed are the women who can't have children! Blessed are those who never gave birth or fed babies!' It is written,

> " 'The people will say to the mountains, "Fall
> on us!"
> They'll say to the hills, "Cover us!" ' "

(from the prophet Hosea)

People do these things when trees are green. So what will happen when trees are dry?"

Two other men were also led out with Jesus to be

killed. Both of them had broken the law. The soldiers brought them to the place called the Skull. There they

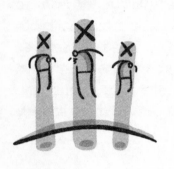

nailed Jesus to the cross. He hung between the two criminals. One was on his right and one was on his left. Jesus said, "Father, forgive them. They don't know what they are doing." The soldiers divided up his clothes by casting lots.

The people stood there watching. The rulers even made fun of Jesus. They said, "He saved others. Let him save himself if he is God's Messiah, the Chosen One."

The soldiers also came up and poked fun at him. They offered him wine vinegar. They said, "If you are the king of the Jews, save yourself."

A written sign had been placed above him. It read,

THIS IS THE KING OF THE JEWS.

One of the criminals hanging there made fun of Jesus. He said, "Aren't you the Messiah? Save yourself! Save us!"

But the other criminal scolded him. "Don't you have any respect for God?" he said. "Remember, you are under the same sentence of death. We are being punished fairly. We are getting just what our actions call for. But this man hasn't done anything wrong."

Then he said, "Jesus, remember me when you come into your kingdom."

Jesus answered him, "What I'm about to tell you is true. Today you will be with me in paradise."

It was now about noon. Then darkness covered the whole land until three o'clock. The sun had stopped shining. The temple curtain was torn in two. Jesus called out in a loud voice, "Father, into your hands I commit my life." After he said this, he took his last breath.

The Roman commander saw what had happened. He praised God and said, "Jesus was surely a man who did what was right." The people had gathered to watch this sight. When they saw what happened, they felt very sad. Then they went away. But all those who knew Jesus stood not very far away, watching these things. They included the women who had followed him from Galilee.

A man named Joseph was a member of the Jewish Council. He was a good and honest man. Joseph had not agreed with what the leaders had decided and

done. He was from Arimathea, a town in Judea. He himself was waiting for God's kingdom. Joseph went to Pilate and asked for Jesus' body. Joseph took it down and wrapped it in linen cloth. Then he placed it in a tomb cut in the rock. No-one had ever been buried there. It was Preparation Day. The Sabbath day was about to begin.

The women who had come with Jesus from Galilee followed Joseph. They saw the tomb and how Jesus' body was placed in it. Then they went home. There they prepared spices and perfumes. But they rested on the Sabbath day in order to obey the Law.

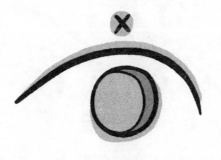

It was very early in the morning on the first day of the week. The women took the spices they had prepared. Then they went to the tomb. They found the stone rolled away from it. When they entered the tomb,

they did not find the body of the Lord Jesus. They were wondering about this. Suddenly two men in clothes as bright as lightning stood beside them. The women were terrified. They bowed down with their faces to the ground. Then the men said to them, "Why do you look for the living among the dead? Jesus is not here! He has risen! Remember how he told you he would rise. It was while he was still with you in Galilee. He said, 'The Son of Man must be handed over to sinful people. He must be nailed to a cross. On the third day he will rise from the dead.'" Then the women remembered Jesus' words.

They came back from the tomb. They told all these things to the 11 apostles and to all the others. Mary Magdalene, Joanna, Mary the mother of James, and the others with them were the ones who told the apostles. But the apostles did not believe the women. Their words didn't make any sense to them. But Peter got up and ran to the tomb. He bent over and saw the strips of linen lying by themselves. Then he went away, wondering what had happened.

That same day two of Jesus' followers were going to a village called Emmaus. It was about seven miles from Jerusalem. They were talking with each other about everything that had happened. As they talked about those things, Jesus himself came up and walked along with them. But God kept them from recognising him.

Jesus asked them, "What are you talking about as you walk along?"

They stood still, and their faces were sad. One of them was named Cleopas. He said to Jesus, "Are you the only person visiting Jerusalem who doesn't know? Don't you know about the things that have happened there in the last few days?"

"What things?" Jesus asked.

"About Jesus of Nazareth," they replied. "He was a prophet. He was powerful in what he said and did in the sight of God and all the people. The chief priests and our rulers handed Jesus over to be sentenced to death. They nailed him to a cross. But we had hoped that he was the one who was going to set Israel free. Also, it is the third day since all this happened. Some of our women amazed us too. Early this morning they went to the tomb. But they didn't find his body. So they came and told us what they had seen. They saw angels, who said Jesus was alive. Then some of our friends went to the tomb. They saw it was empty, just as the women had said. They didn't see Jesus' body there."

Jesus said to them, "How foolish you are! How long it takes you to believe all that the prophets said! Didn't the Messiah have to suffer these things and then receive his glory?" Jesus explained to them what was said about himself in all the Scriptures. He began with Moses and all the Prophets.

They approached the village where they were going. Jesus kept walking

as if he were going further. But they tried hard to keep him from leaving. They said, "Stay with us. It is nearly evening. The day is almost over." So he went in to stay with them.

He joined them at the table. Then he took bread and gave thanks. He broke it and began to give it to them. Their eyes were opened, and they recognised him. But then he disappeared from their sight. They said to each other, "He explained to us what the Scriptures meant. Weren't we excited as he talked with us on the road?"

They got up and returned at once to Jerusalem. There they found the 11 disciples and those with them. They were all gathered together. They were saying, "It's true! The Lord has risen! He has appeared to Simon!" Then the two of them told what had happened to them on the way. They told how they had recognised Jesus when he broke the bread.

The disciples were still talking about this when Jesus himself suddenly stood among them. He said, "May you have peace!"

They were surprised and terrified. They thought they were seeing a ghost. Jesus said to them, "Why are you troubled? Why do you have doubts in your minds? Look at my hands and my feet. It's really me! Touch me and see. A ghost does not have a body or bones. But you can see that I do."

After he said that, he showed them his hands and feet. But they still did not believe it. They were amazed and filled with joy. So Jesus asked them, "Do you have anything here to eat?" They gave him a piece of cooked fish. He took it and ate it in front of them.

Jesus said to them, "This is what I told you while I was still with you. Everything written about me in the Law of Moses, the Prophets and the Psalms must come true."

Then he opened their minds so they could understand the Scriptures. He told them, "This is what is written. The Messiah will suffer. He will rise from the dead on the third day. His followers will preach in his name. They will tell others to turn away from their sins and be forgiven. People from every nation will hear it, beginning at Jerusalem. You have seen these things with your own eyes. I am going to send you what my Father has promised. But for now, stay in the city. Stay there until you have received power from heaven."

Jesus led his disciples out to the area near Bethany. Then he lifted up his hands and blessed them. While he was blessing them, he left them. He was taken up into heaven. Then they worshipped him. With great joy, they returned to Jerusalem. Every day they went to the temple, praising God.

♔ Five ♔

Theophilus, I wrote about Jesus in my earlier book. I wrote about all he did and taught until the day he was taken up to heaven. Before Jesus left, he gave orders to the apostles he had chosen. He did this through the Holy Spirit. After his suffering and death, he appeared to them. In many ways he proved that he was alive. He appeared to them over a period of 40 days. During that time he spoke about God's kingdom. One day Jesus was eating with them. He gave them a command. "Do not leave Jerusalem," he said. "Wait for the gift my Father promised. You have heard me talk about it. John baptised with water. But in a few days you will be baptised with the Holy Spirit."

Then the apostles gathered around Jesus and asked him a question. "Lord," they said, "are you going to give the kingdom back to Israel now?"

He said to them, "You should not be concerned about times or dates. The Father has set them by his own authority. But you will receive power when the Holy Spirit comes on you. Then you will tell people about me in Jerusalem, and in all Judea and Samaria. And you will even tell other people about me from one end of the earth to the other."

After Jesus said this, he was taken up to heaven. The apostles watched until a cloud hid him from their sight.

While he was going up, they kept on looking at the sky. Suddenly two men dressed in white clothing stood beside them. "Men of Galilee," they said, "why do you

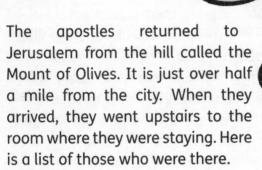

stand here looking at the sky? Jesus has been taken away from you into heaven. But he will come back in the same way you saw him go."

The apostles returned to Jerusalem from the hill called the Mount of Olives. It is just over half a mile from the city. When they arrived, they went upstairs to the room where they were staying. Here is a list of those who were there.

> Peter, John, James and Andrew,
> Philip and Thomas,
> Bartholomew and Matthew,
> James son of Alphaeus, Simon the Zealot and Judas son of James

They all came together regularly to pray. The women joined them too. So did Jesus' mother Mary and his brothers.

In those days Peter stood up among the believers. About 120 of them were there. Peter said, "Brothers and sisters, a long time ago the Holy Spirit spoke through David. He spoke about Judas Iscariot. What the Scripture said would happen had to come true. Judas was the guide for the men who arrested Jesus. But Judas was one of us. He shared with us in our work for God."

Judas bought a field with the payment he received for the evil thing he had done. He fell down headfirst in the field. His body burst open. All his insides spilled out. Everyone in Jerusalem heard about this. So they called that field Akeldama. In their language, Akeldama means the Field of Blood.

Peter said, "Here is what is written in the Book of Psalms. It says,

"'May his home be deserted.
    May no-one live in it.'   *(from Psalm 69)*

The Psalms also say,

"'Let someone else take his place as leader.'
    (from Psalm 109)

So we need to choose someone to take his place. It will have to be a man who was with us the whole time the Lord Jesus was living among us. That time began when John was baptising. It ended when Jesus was taken up from us. The one we choose must join us in telling people that Jesus rose from the dead."

So they suggested the names of two men. One was Joseph, who was called Barsabbas. He was also called Justus. The other man was Matthias. Then the believers prayed. They said, "Lord, you know everyone's heart. Show us which of these two you have chosen. Show us who should take the place of Judas as an apostle. He gave up being an apostle to go where he belongs." Then they cast lots. Matthias was chosen. So he was added to the 11 apostles.

When the day of Pentecost came, all the believers gathered in one place. Suddenly a sound came from heaven. It was like a strong wind blowing. It filled the whole house where they were sitting. They saw something that looked like fire in the shape of tongues. The flames separated and came to rest on each of them. All of them were filled with the Holy Spirit. They began to speak in languages they had not known before. The Spirit gave them the ability to do this.

Godly Jews from every country in the world were staying in Jerusalem. A crowd came together when they heard the sound. They were bewildered because each of them heard their own language being spoken.

The crowd was really amazed. They asked, "Aren't all these people who are speaking Galileans? Then why do we each hear them speaking in our own native language? We are Parthians, Medes and Elamites. We live in Mesopotamia, Judea and Cappadocia. We are from Pontus, Asia, Phrygia and Pamphylia. Others of us are from Egypt and the parts of Libya near Cyrene. Still others are visitors from Rome. Some of the visitors are Jews. Others have accepted the Jewish faith. Also, Cretans and Arabs are here. We hear all these people speaking about God's wonders in our own languages!" They were amazed and bewildered. They asked one another, "What does this mean?"

But some people in the crowd made fun of the believers. "They've had too much wine!" they said.

Then Peter stood up with the 11 apostles. In a loud voice he spoke to the crowd. "My fellow Jews," he said, "let me explain this to you. All of you who live in Jerusalem, listen carefully to what I say. You think these people are drunk. But they aren't. It's only nine o'clock in the morning! No, here is what the prophet Joel meant. He said,

"'In the last days, God says,
I will pour out my Holy Spirit on all people.
Your sons and daughters will prophesy.
Your young men will see visions.
Your old men will have dreams.
In those days, I will pour out my Spirit on my
servants.

I will pour out my Spirit on both men and
women.
When I do, they will prophesy.
I will show wonders in the heavens above.
I will show signs on the earth below.
There will be blood and fire and clouds of
smoke.
The sun will become dark.
The moon will turn red like blood.
This will happen before the coming of the
great and glorious day of the Lord.
Everyone who calls
on the name of the Lord will be saved.'

(from the prophet Joel)

"Fellow Israelites, listen to this! Jesus of Nazareth
was a man who had God's approval. God did miracles,
wonders and signs among you through Jesus. You
yourselves know this. Long ago God planned that
Jesus would be handed over to you. With the help of
evil people, you put Jesus to death. You nailed him to
the cross. But God raised him from the dead. He set
him free from the suffering of death. It wasn't possible
for death to keep its hold on Jesus. David spoke about
him. He said,

"'I know that the Lord is always with me.
Because he is at my right hand,
I will always be secure.
So my heart is glad and joy is on my tongue.
My whole body will be full of hope.

You will not leave me in the place of the dead.
  You will not let your holy one rot away.
You always show me the path that leads to life.
  You will fill me with joy when I am with you.'

(from Psalm 16)

"Fellow Israelites, you can be sure that King David died. He was buried. His tomb is still here today. But David was a prophet. He knew that God had made a promise to him. God had promised that he would make someone in David's family line king after him. David saw what was coming. So he spoke about the Messiah rising from the dead. He said that the Messiah would not be left in the place of the dead. His body wouldn't rot in the ground. God has raised this same Jesus back to life. We are all witnesses of this. Jesus has been given a place of honour at the right hand of God. He has received the Holy

Spirit from the Father. This is what God had promised. It is Jesus who has poured out what you now see and hear. David did not go up to heaven. But he said,

> "'The Lord said to my Lord,
>   "Sit at my right hand.
> I will put your enemies
>   under your control."'   *(from Psalm 110)*

"So be sure of this, all you people of Israel. You nailed Jesus to the cross. But God has made him both Lord and Messiah."

When the people heard this, it had a deep effect on them. They said to Peter and the other apostles, "Brothers, what should we do?"

Peter replied, "All of you must turn away from your sins and be baptised in the name of Jesus Christ. Then your sins will be forgiven. You will receive the gift of the Holy Spirit. The promise is for you and your children. It is also for all who are far away. It is for all whom the Lord our God will choose."

Peter said many other things to warn them. He

begged them, "Save yourselves from these evil people." Those who accepted his message were baptised. About 3,000 people joined the believers that day.

The believers studied what the apostles taught. They shared their lives together. They ate and prayed together. Everyone was amazed at what God was doing. They were amazed when the apostles performed many wonders and signs. All the believers were together. They shared everything they had. They sold property and other things they owned. They gave to anyone who needed something. Every day they met together in the temple courtyard. They ate meals together in their homes. Their hearts were glad and sincere. They praised God. They were respected by all the people. Every day the Lord added to their group those who were being saved.

One day Peter and John were going up to the temple. It was three o'clock in the afternoon. It was the time for prayer. A man unable to walk was being carried to the temple gate called Beautiful. He had been that way since he was born. Every day someone put him near the gate.

There he would beg from people going into the temple courtyards. He saw that Peter and John were about to enter. So he asked them for money. Peter looked straight at him, and so did John. Then Peter said, "Look at us!" So the man watched them closely. He expected to get something from them.

Peter said, "I don't have any silver or gold. But I'll give you what I do have. In the name of Jesus Christ of Nazareth, get up and walk." Then Peter took him by the right hand and helped him up. At once the man's feet and ankles became strong. He jumped to his feet and began to walk. He went with Peter and John into the temple courtyards. He walked and jumped and praised God. All the people saw him walking and praising God. They recognised him as the same man who used to sit and beg at the temple gate called Beautiful. They were filled with wonder. They were amazed at what had happened to him.

The man was holding on to Peter and John. All the people were amazed. They came running to them at the place called Solomon's Porch. When Peter saw this, he said, "Fellow Israelites, why does this surprise you? Why do you stare at us? It's not as if we've made this man walk by our own power or godliness. The God of our fathers, Abraham, Isaac and Jacob, has done this. God has brought glory to Jesus, who serves him. But you handed Jesus over to be killed. Pilate had decided to let him go. But you spoke against Jesus when he was in Pilate's court. You spoke against the Holy and Blameless One. You asked for a murderer to be set free instead. You killed the one who gives life. But God raised him from the dead. We are witnesses of this. This man whom you see and know was made strong because of faith in Jesus' name. Faith in Jesus has healed him completely. You can see it with your own eyes.

"My fellow Israelites, I know you didn't realise what you were doing. Neither did your leaders. But God had given a promise through all the prophets. And this is how he has made his promise come true. He said that his Messiah would suffer. So turn away from your sins. Turn to God. Then your sins will be wiped away. The time will come when the Lord will make everything new. He will send the Messiah. Jesus has been appointed as the Messiah for you. Heaven must receive him until the time when God makes everything new. He promised this long ago through his holy prophets. Moses said, 'The Lord your God will raise up for you a prophet like me. He will be one of your own people. You must listen to everything he tells you. Anyone who does not listen to him will be completely cut off from their people.'

(from the Book of Deuteronomy)

"Beginning with Samuel, all the prophets spoke about this. They said these days would come. What the prophets said was meant for you. The covenant God made with your people long ago is yours also. He said to Abraham, 'All nations on earth will be blessed through your children.' *(from the Book of Genesis)* God raised up Jesus, who serves him. God sent him first to you. He

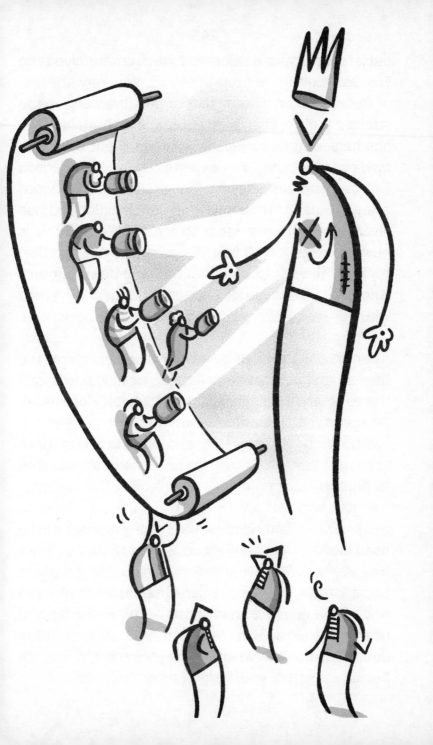

did it to bless you. He wanted to turn each of you from your evil ways."

Peter and John were speaking to the people. The priests, the captain of the temple guard, and the Sadducees came up to the apostles. They were very upset by what the apostles were teaching the people. The apostles were saying that people can be raised from the dead. They said this can happen because Jesus rose from the dead. So the temple authorities arrested Peter and John. It was already evening, so they put them in prison until the next day. But many who heard the message believed. The number of men who believed grew to about 5,000.

The next day the rulers, the elders and the teachers of the law met in Jerusalem. Annas, the high priest, was there. So were Caiaphas, John, Alexander and other people in the high priest's family. They had Peter and John brought to them. They wanted to question them. "By what power did you do this?" they asked. "And through whose name?"

Peter was filled with the Holy Spirit. He said to them, "Rulers and elders of the people! Are you asking us to explain our actions today? Do you want to know why we were kind to a man who couldn't walk? Are you asking how he was healed? Then listen to this, you and all the people of Israel! You nailed Jesus Christ of Nazareth to the cross. But God raised him from the dead. It is through Jesus' name that this man stands healed in front of you. Scripture says that Jesus is

" 'the stone you builders did not accept.
  But it has become the most important stone
  of all.' *(from Psalm 118)*

You can't be saved by believing in anyone else. God has given people no other name under heaven that will save them."

The leaders saw how bold Peter and John were. They also realised that Peter and John were ordinary men with no training. This surprised the leaders. They realised that these men had been with Jesus. The leaders could see the man who had been healed. He was standing there with them. So there was nothing they could say. They ordered Peter and John to leave the Sanhedrin. Then they talked things over. "What can we do with these men?" they asked. "Everyone living in Jerusalem knows they have performed an unusual miracle. We can't say it didn't happen. We have to stop this thing. It must not spread any further among the people. We have to warn these men. They must never speak to anyone in Jesus' name again."

Once again the leaders called in Peter and John. They commanded them not to speak or teach at all in Jesus' name. But Peter and John replied, "Which is right from God's point of view? Should we listen to you? Or should we listen to God? You be the judges! There's nothing else we can do. We have to speak about the things we've seen and heard."

The leaders warned them again. Then they let them go. They couldn't decide how to punish Peter and John. They knew that all the people were praising God for what had happened. The man who had been healed by the miracle was over 40 years old.

Peter and John were allowed to leave. They went back to their own people. They reported everything the chief priests and the elders had said to them. The believers heard this. Then they raised their voices together in prayer to God. "Lord and King," they said, "you made the heavens, the earth and the sea. You made everything in them. Long ago you spoke by the Holy Spirit. You spoke through the mouth of our father David, who served you. You said,

"'Why are the nations angry?
    Why do the people make useless plans?
The kings of the earth rise up.
    The rulers of the earth gather together
against the Lord
    and against his anointed king.'   *(from Psalm 2)*

"In fact, Herod and Pontius Pilate met with the Gentiles in this city. They also met with the people of Israel. All of them made plans against your holy servant Jesus. He is the one you anointed. They did what your power and purpose had already decided should happen. Now, Lord, consider the bad things they say they are going to do. Help us to be very bold when we speak your word. Stretch out your hand to heal. Do signs and wonders through the name of your holy servant Jesus."

After they prayed, the place where they were meeting was shaken. They were all filled with the Holy Spirit. They were bold when they spoke God's word.

All the believers were agreed in heart and mind. They didn't claim that anything they had was their own. Instead, they shared everything they owned. With great power the apostles continued their teaching. They were telling people that the Lord Jesus had risen from the dead. And God's grace was working powerfully in all of them. So there were no needy people among them. From time to time, those who owned land or houses sold them. They brought the money from the sales. They put it down at the apostles' feet. It was then given out to anyone who needed it.

Joseph was a Levite from Cyprus. The apostles called him Barnabas. The name Barnabas means Son of Help. Barnabas sold a field he owned. He brought the money from the sale. He put it down at the apostles' feet.

A man named Ananias and his wife, Sapphira, also sold some land. He kept part of the money for himself. Sapphira knew he had kept it. He brought the rest of it and put it down at the apostles' feet.

Then Peter said, "Ananias, why did you let Satan fill your heart? He made you lie to the Holy Spirit. You have kept some of the money you received for the land. Didn't the land belong to you before it was sold? After

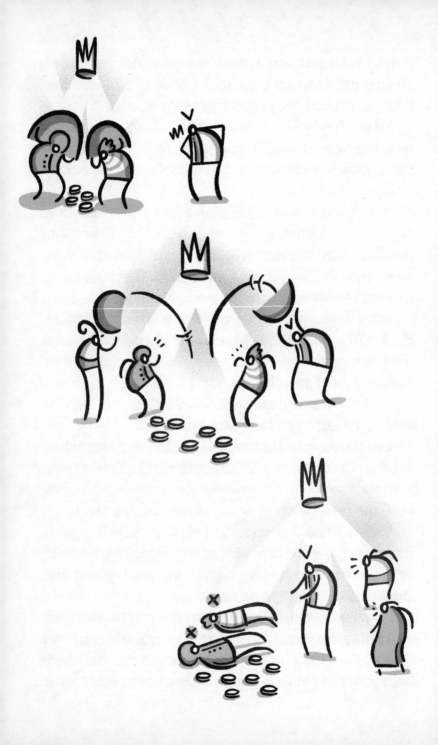

it was sold, you could have used the money as you wished. What made you think of doing such a thing? You haven't lied just to people. You've also lied to God."

When Ananias heard this, he fell down and died. All who heard what had happened were filled with fear. Some young men came and wrapped up his body. They carried him out and buried him.

About three hours later, the wife of Ananias came in. She didn't know what had happened. Peter asked her, "Tell me. Is this the price you and Ananias sold the land for?"

"Yes," she said. "That's the price."

Peter asked her, "How could you agree to test the Spirit of the Lord? Listen! You can hear the steps of the men who buried your husband. They are at the door. They will carry you out also."

At that moment she fell down at Peter's feet and died. Then the young men came in. They saw that Sapphira was dead. So they carried her out and buried her beside her husband. The whole church and all who heard about these things were filled with fear.

The apostles did many signs and wonders among the people. All the believers used to meet together at Solomon's Porch. No outsider dared to join them. But the people thought highly of them. More and more men and women believed in the Lord. They joined the other believers. So people brought those who were ill into the streets. They placed them on beds and mats. They hoped that at least Peter's shadow might fall on some of them as he walked by. Crowds even gathered from the towns around Jerusalem. They brought their ill people. They also brought those who were suffering because of evil spirits. All of them were healed.

The high priest and all his companions were Sadducees. They were very jealous of the apostles. So they arrested them and put them in the public jail. But during the night an angel of the Lord came. He opened the doors of the jail and brought the apostles out. "Go! Stand in the temple courtyard," the angel said. "Tell the people all about this new life."

Early the next day they did as they had been told. They entered the temple courtyard. There they began to teach the people.

The high priest and his companions arrived. They called the Sanhedrin together. The Sanhedrin was a gathering of all the elders of Israel. They sent for the apostles who were in jail. The officers arrived at the jail. But they didn't find the apostles there. So they went back and reported it. "We found the jail locked up tight," they said. "The guards were standing at the doors. But when we opened the doors, we didn't find anyone inside." When the captain of the temple guard and the chief priests heard this report, they were bewildered. They wondered what would happen next.

Then someone came and said, "Look! The men you put in jail are standing in the temple courtyard. They are teaching the people." So the captain went with his officers and brought the apostles back. But they didn't use force. They were afraid the people would kill them by throwing stones at them.

They brought the apostles to the Sanhedrin. The high priest questioned them. "We gave you clear orders not to teach in Jesus' name," he said. "But you have filled Jerusalem with your teaching. You want to make us guilty of this man's death."

Peter and the other apostles replied, "We must obey God instead of people! You had Jesus killed by nailing him to a cross. But the God of our people raised Jesus from the dead. Now Jesus is Prince and Saviour. God has proved this by giving Jesus a place of honour with him. He did it to turn Israel away from their sins and forgive them. We are telling people about these things. And so is the Holy Spirit. God has given the Spirit to those who obey him."

When the leaders heard this, they became very angry. They wanted to put the apostles to death. But a Pharisee named Gamaliel stood up in the Sanhedrin. He was a teacher of the law. He was honoured by all the people. He ordered the apostles to be taken outside for a little while. Then Gamaliel spoke to the Sanhedrin. "Men of Israel," he said, "think carefully about what you plan to do to these men. Some time ago Theudas appeared. He claimed he was really somebody. About 400 people followed him. But he was killed. All his followers were scattered. So they accomplished nothing. After this, Judas from Galilee came along. This was in the days when the Romans made a list of all the people. Judas led a gang of men against the Romans. He too was killed. All his followers were scattered. So let me give you some advice. Leave these men alone! Let them go! If their plans and actions only come from people, they will fail. But if their plans come from God, you won't be able to stop these men. You will only find yourselves fighting against God."

His speech won the leaders over. They called the apostles in and had them whipped. The leaders ordered them not to speak in Jesus' name. Then they let the apostles go.

The apostles were full of joy as they left the Sanhedrin. They considered it an honour to suffer shame for the name of Jesus. Everyday they taught in the temple courtyards and from house to house. They never stopped telling people the good news that Jesus is the Messiah.

In those days the number of believers was growing. The Greek Jews complained about the non-Greek Jews. They said that the widows of the Greek Jews were not being taken care of. They weren't getting their fair share of food each day. So the 12 apostles gathered all the believers together. They said, "It wouldn't be right for us to give up teaching God's word. And we'd have to stop teaching to wait on tables. Brothers and sisters, choose seven of your men. They must be known as men who are wise and full of the Holy Spirit. We will turn this important work over to them. Then we can give our attention to prayer and to teaching God's word."

This plan pleased the whole group. They chose Stephen. He was full of faith and of the Holy Spirit. Philip, Procorus, Nicanor, Timon and Parmenas were chosen too. The group also chose Nicolas from Antioch. He had accepted the Jewish faith. The group brought them to the apostles. Then the apostles prayed and placed their hands on them.

So God's word spread. The number of believers in Jerusalem grew quickly. Also, a large number of priests began to obey Jesus' teachings.

♔ Six ♔

Stephen was full of God's grace and power. He did great wonders and signs among the people. But members of the group called the Synagogue of the Freedmen began to oppose him. Some of them were Jews from Cyrene and Alexandria. Others were Jews from Cilicia and Asia Minor. They all began to argue with Stephen. But he was too wise for them. That's because the Holy Spirit gave Stephen wisdom whenever he spoke.

Then in secret they talked some men into lying about Stephen. They said, "We heard Stephen speak evil things against Moses and against God."

So the people were stirred up. The elders and the teachers of the law were stirred up too. They arrested Stephen and brought him to the Sanhedrin. They found witnesses who were willing to tell lies. These liars said, "This fellow never stops speaking against this holy place. He also speaks against the law. We have heard him say that this Jesus of Nazareth will destroy this place. He says Jesus will change the practices that Moses handed down to us."

All who were sitting in the Sanhedrin looked right at Stephen. They saw that his face was like the face of an angel.

Then the high priest questioned Stephen. "Is what these people are saying true?" he asked.

"Brothers and fathers, listen to me!" Stephen replied. "The God of glory appeared to our father Abraham. At that time Abraham was still in Mesopotamia. He had not yet begun living in Harran. 'Leave your country and your people,' God said. 'Go to the land I will show you.' *(from the Book of Genesis)*

"So Abraham left the land of Babylonia. He settled in Harran. After his father died, God sent Abraham to this land where you are now living. God didn't give him any property here. He didn't even give him enough land to set his foot on. But God made a promise to him and to all his family after him. He said they would possess the land. The promise was made even though at that time Abraham had no child. Here is what God said to him. 'For 400 years your family after you will be strangers in a country not their own. They will be slaves and will be treated badly. But I will punish the nation that makes them slaves,' God said. 'After that, they will leave that country and worship me here.' *(from the Book of Genesis)* Then God made a covenant with Abraham. God told him that circumcision would show who the members of the covenant were. Abraham became Isaac's father. He circumcised Isaac eight days after he was born. Later, Isaac became Jacob's father. Jacob had 12 sons. They became the founders of the 12 tribes of Israel.

"Jacob's sons were jealous of their brother Joseph. So they sold him as a slave. He was taken to Egypt. But God was with him. He saved Joseph from all his troubles. God made Joseph wise. He helped him to become the friend of Pharaoh, the king of Egypt. So Pharaoh made Joseph ruler over Egypt and his whole palace.

"There was not enough food for all Egypt and Canaan. This brought great suffering. Jacob and his sons couldn't find food. But Jacob heard that there was corn in Egypt. So he sent his sons on their first visit. On their second visit, Joseph told his brothers who he was. Pharaoh learned about Joseph's family. After this, Joseph sent for his father Jacob and his whole family. The total number of people was 75. Then Jacob went down to Egypt. There he and his family died. Some of their bodies were brought back to Shechem. They were placed in a tomb Abraham had bought. He had purchased it from Hamor's sons at Shechem. He had purchased it for a certain amount of money.

"In Egypt the number of our people grew and grew. It was nearly time for God to make his promise to Abraham come true. Then 'a new king came to power in Egypt. Joseph didn't mean anything to him.' *(from the*

(400)

Book of Exodus) The king was very evil and dishonest with our people. He treated them badly. He forced them to throw out their newborn babies to die.

"At that time Moses was born. He was not an ordinary child. For three months he was taken care of by his family. Then he was placed outside. But Pharaoh's daughter took him home. She brought him up as her own son. Moses was taught all the knowledge of the people of Egypt. He became a powerful speaker and a man of action.

"When Moses was 40 years old, he decided to visit the people of Israel. They were his own people. He saw one of them being treated badly by an Egyptian. So he went to help him. He got even by killing the man. Moses thought his own people would realise that God was using him to save them. But they didn't. The next day Moses saw two Israelites fighting. He tried to make peace between them. 'Men, you are both Israelites,' he said. 'Why do you want to hurt each other?'

"But the man who was treating the other one badly pushed Moses to one side. He said, 'Who made you ruler and judge over us? Are you thinking of killing me as you killed the Egyptian yesterday?' *(from the Book of Exodus)* When Moses heard this, he escaped to Midian. He lived there as an outsider. He became the father of two sons there.

"Forty years passed. Then an angel appeared to Moses in the flames of a burning bush. This happened in the desert near Mount Sinai. When Moses saw the bush, he was amazed. He went over for a closer look.

There he heard the Lord say, 'I am the God of your fathers. I am the God of Abraham, Isaac and Jacob.' *(from the Book of Exodus)* **Moses shook with fear. He didn't dare to look.**

"Then the Lord said to him, 'Take off your sandals. You must do this because the place where you are standing is holy ground. I have seen my people beaten down in Egypt. I have heard their groans. I have come down to set them free. Now come. I will send you back to Egypt.' *(from the Book of Exodus)*

"This is the same Moses the two men of Israel would not accept. They had said, 'Who made you ruler and judge?' But God himself sent Moses to rule the people of Israel and set them free. He spoke to Moses through an angel. The angel had appeared to him in the bush. So Moses led them out of Egypt. He did wonders and signs in Egypt, at the Red Sea, and for 40 years in the desert.

"This is the same Moses who spoke to the Israelites. 'God will send you a prophet,' he said. 'He will be like me. He will come from your own people.' *(from the Book of Deuteronomy)* **Moses was with the Israelites in the desert.**

He was with the angel who spoke to him on Mount Sinai. Moses was with our people of long ago. He received living words to pass on to us.

"But our people refused to obey Moses. They would not accept him. In their hearts, they wished they were back in Egypt. They told Aaron, 'Make us a god who will lead us. This fellow Moses brought us up out of Egypt. But we don't know what has happened to him!' *(from the Book of Exodus)* That was the time they made a statue to be their god. It was shaped like a calf. They brought sacrifices to it. They even enjoyed what they had made with their own hands. But God turned away from them. He let them go on worshipping the sun, moon and stars. This agrees with what is written in the book of the prophets. There it says,

> "'People of Israel, did you bring me sacrifices
>   and offerings
>   for 40 years in the desert?
> You have taken with you the shrine of your
>   false god Molek.

You have taken with you the star of your
false god Rephan.
You made statues of those gods to worship.
So I will send you away from your country.'

(from the prophet Amos)

God sent them to Babylon and even further.

"Long ago our people were in the desert. They had with them the holy tent. The tent was where the tablets of the covenant law were kept. Moses had made the holy tent as God had commanded him. Moses made it like the pattern he had seen. Our people received the tent from God. Then they brought it with them when they took the land of Canaan. God drove out the nations that were in their way. At that time Joshua was Israel's leader. "The tent remained in the land until David's time. David was blessed by God. So David asked if he could build a house for the God of Jacob. But it was Solomon who built the temple for God.

"But the Most High God does not live in houses made by human hands. As God says through the prophet,

"'Heaven is my throne.
The earth is under my control.
What kind of house will you build for me?
says the Lord.
Where will my resting place be?
Didn't my hand make all these things?'

(from the prophet Isaiah)

"You stubborn people! You won't obey! You won't listen! You are just like your people of long ago! You

always oppose the Holy Spirit! Was there ever a prophet your people didn't try to hurt? They even killed those who told about the coming of the Blameless One. And now you have handed him over to his enemies. You have murdered him. The law you received was given by angels. But you haven't obeyed it."

When the members of the Sanhedrin heard this, they became very angry. They were so angry they ground their teeth at Stephen. But he was full of the Holy Spirit. He looked up to heaven and saw God's glory. He saw Jesus standing at God's right hand. "Look!" he said. "I see heaven open. The Son of Man is standing at God's right hand."

When the Sanhedrin heard this, they covered their ears. They yelled at the top of their voices. They all rushed at him. They dragged him out of the city. They began to throw stones at him to kill him. The people who had brought false charges against Stephen took off their coats. They placed them at the feet of a young man named Saul.

While the members of the Sanhedrin were throwing stones at Stephen, he prayed. "Lord Jesus, receive my spirit," he said. Then he fell on his knees. He cried out, "Lord! Don't hold this sin against them!" When he had said this, he died.

And Saul had agreed with the Sanhedrin that Stephen should die.

On that day the church in Jerusalem began to be attacked and treated badly. All except the apostles were scattered throughout Judea and Samaria. Godly Jews buried Stephen. They mourned deeply for him. But Saul began to destroy the church. He went from house to house. He dragged away men and women and put them in prison.

The believers who had been scattered preached the word everywhere they went. Philip went down to a city in Samaria. There he preached about the Messiah. The crowds listened to Philip and saw the signs he did. All of them paid close attention to what he said. Evil spirits screamed and came out of many people. Many people who were disabled or who couldn't walk were healed. So there was great joy in that city.

A man named Simon lived in the city. For quite a while he had practised evil magic there. He amazed all the people of Samaria. He claimed to be someone great. And all the people listened to him, from the least important of them to the most important. They exclaimed, "It is right to call this man the Great Power of God!" He had amazed them for a long time with his evil magic. So they followed him. But Philip announced the good news of God's kingdom and the name of

Jesus Christ. So men and women believed and were baptised. Simon himself believed and was baptised. He followed Philip everywhere. He was amazed by the great signs and miracles he saw.

The apostles in Jerusalem heard that people in Samaria had accepted God's word. So they sent Peter and John to Samaria. When they arrived there, they prayed for the new believers. They prayed that they would receive the Holy Spirit. The Holy Spirit had not yet come on any of them. They had only been baptised in the name of the Lord Jesus. Then Peter and John placed their hands on them. And they received the Holy Spirit.

Simon watched as the apostles placed their hands on them. He saw that the Spirit was given to them. So he offered money to Peter and John. He said, "Give me this power too. Then everyone I place my hands on will receive the Holy Spirit."

Peter answered, "May your money be destroyed with you! Do you think you can buy God's gift with money? You have no part or share in this holy work. Your heart is not right with God. Turn away from this evil sin of yours. Pray to the Lord. Perhaps he will forgive you for having such a thought in your heart. I see that you are very bitter. You are a prisoner of sin."

Then Simon answered, "Pray to the Lord for me. Pray that nothing you have said will happen to me."

Peter and John continued to preach the word of the Lord and tell people about Jesus. Then they returned to Jerusalem. On the way they preached the good news in many villages in Samaria.

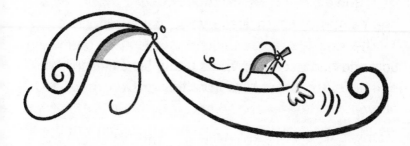

An angel of the Lord spoke to Philip. "Go south to the desert road," he said. "It's the road that goes down from Jerusalem to Gaza." So Philip started out. On his way he met an Ethiopian official. The man had an important position in charge of all the wealth of the Kandake. Kandake means queen of Ethiopia. This official had gone to Jerusalem to worship. On his way home he was sitting in his chariot. He was reading the Book of Isaiah the prophet. The Holy Spirit told Philip, "Go to that chariot. Stay near it."

So Philip ran up to the chariot. He heard the man reading Isaiah the prophet. "Do you understand what you're reading?" Philip asked.

"How can I?" he said. "I need someone to explain it to me." So he invited Philip to come up and sit with him.

Here is the part of Scripture the official was reading. It says,

"He was led like a sheep to be killed.

Just as lambs are silent while their wool is
being cut off,
he did not open his mouth.
When he was treated badly, he was refused a
fair trial.
Who can say anything about his children?
His life was cut off from the earth." *(from the*
prophet Isaiah)

The official said to Philip, "Tell me, please. Who is the prophet talking about? Himself, or someone else?" Then Philip began with that same part of Scripture. He told him the good news about Jesus.

As they travelled along the road, they came to some water. The official said, "Look! Here is water! What can stop me from being baptised?" He gave orders to stop the chariot. Then both Philip and the official went down into the water. Philip baptised him. When they came up out of the water, the Spirit of the Lord suddenly took Philip away. The official did not see him again. He went on his way full of joy. Philip was seen next at Azotus. From there he travelled all around. He preached the good news in all the towns. Finally he arrived in Caesarea.

Meanwhile, Saul continued to oppose the Lord's followers. He said they would be put to death. He went to the high priest. He asked the priest for letters to the synagogues in Damascus. He wanted to find men and women who belonged to the Way of Jesus. The letters would allow him to take them as prisoners to Jerusalem. On his journey, Saul approached Damascus. Suddenly a light from heaven flashed around him. He fell to the ground. He heard a voice speak to him, "Saul! Saul! Why are you opposing me?"

"Who are you, Lord?" Saul asked.

"I am Jesus," he replied. "I am the one you are opposing. Now get up and go into the city. There you will be told what you must do."

The men travelling with Saul stood there. They weren't able to speak. They had heard the sound. But they didn't see anyone. Saul got up from the ground. He opened his eyes, but he couldn't see. So they led him by the hand into Damascus. For three days he was blind. He didn't eat or drink anything.

In Damascus there was a believer named Ananias. The Lord called out to him in a vision. "Ananias!" he said.

"Yes, Lord," he answered.

The Lord told him, "Go to the house of Judas on Straight Street. Ask for a man from Tarsus named Saul. He is praying. In a vision Saul has seen a man come and place his hands on him. That man's name is Ananias. In the vision, Ananias placed his hands on Saul so he could see again."

"Lord," Ananias answered, "I've heard many reports about this man. They say he has done great harm to your holy people in Jerusalem. Now he has come here to arrest all those who worship you. The chief priests have given him authority to do this."

But the Lord said to Ananias, "Go! I have chosen this man to work for me. He will announce my name to the Gentiles and to their kings. He will also announce my name to the people of Israel. I will show him how much he must suffer for me."

Then Ananias went to the house and entered it. He placed his hands on Saul. "Brother Saul," he said, "you saw the Lord Jesus. He appeared to you on the road as you were coming here. He has sent me so that you will be able to see again. You will be filled with the Holy Spirit." Right away something like scales fell from Saul's eyes. And he could see again. He got up and was baptised. After eating some food, he got his strength back.

Saul spent several days with the believers in Damascus. Right away he began to preach in the synagogues. He taught that Jesus is the Son of God. All who heard him were amazed. They asked, "Isn't he the man who caused great trouble in Jerusalem? Didn't he make trouble for those who worship Jesus? Hasn't he come here to take them as prisoners to the chief priests?" But Saul grew more and more powerful. The Jews living in Damascus couldn't believe what was happening. Saul proved to them that Jesus is the Messiah.

After many days, the Jews had a meeting. They planned to kill Saul. But he learned about their plan. Day and night they watched the city gates closely in order to kill him. But his followers helped him escape by night. They lowered him in a basket through an opening in the wall.

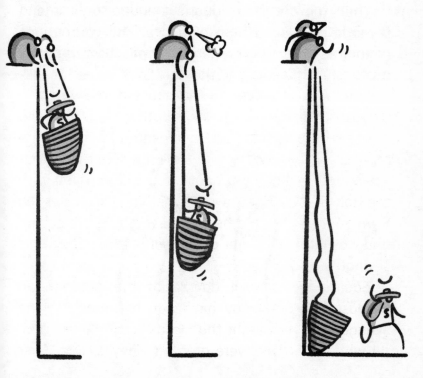

When Saul came to Jerusalem, he tried to join the believers. But they were all afraid of him. They didn't believe he was really one of Jesus' followers. But Barnabas took him to the apostles. He told them about Saul's journey. He said that Saul had seen the Lord. He told how the Lord had spoken to Saul. Barnabas also said that Saul had preached without fear in Jesus' name in Damascus. So Saul stayed with the believers. He moved about freely in Jerusalem. He spoke boldly in the Lord's name. He talked and argued with the Greek Jews. But they tried to kill him. The other believers heard about this. They took Saul down to Caesarea. From there they sent him off to Tarsus.

Then the church throughout Judea, Galilee and Samaria enjoyed a time of peace. The church was strengthened and grew larger. That's because they worshipped the Lord and the Holy Spirit helped them.

♛ Seven ♛

Peter travelled around the country. He went to visit the Lord's people who lived in Lydda. There he found a disabled man named Aeneas. For eight years the man had spent most of his time in bed. "Aeneas," Peter said to him, "Jesus Christ heals you. Get up! Roll up your mat!" So Aeneas got up right away. Everyone who lived in Lydda and Sharon saw him. They turned to the Lord.

In Joppa there was a believer named Tabitha. Her name in the Greek language is Dorcas. She was always doing good and helping poor people. About that time she became ill and died. Her body was washed and placed in a room upstairs. Lydda was near Joppa. The believers heard that Peter was in Lydda. So they sent two men to him. They begged him, "Please come at once!"

Peter went with them. When he arrived, he was taken upstairs to the room. All the widows stood around him crying. They showed him the robes and other clothes Dorcas had made before she died.

Peter sent them all out of the room. Then he got down on his knees and prayed. He turned towards the dead woman. He said, "Tabitha, get up." She opened her eyes. When she saw Peter, she sat up. He took her by the hand and helped her to her feet. Then he called the believers and especially the widows. He brought her to them. They saw that she was alive. This became known all over Joppa. Many people believed in the

Lord. Peter stayed in Joppa for some time. He stayed with Simon, a man who worked with leather.

A man named Cornelius lived in Caesarea. He was a Roman commander in the Italian Regiment. Cornelius and all his family were faithful and worshipped God. He gave freely to people who were in need. He prayed to God regularly. One day about three o'clock in the afternoon he had a vision. He saw clearly an angel of God. The angel came to him and said, "Cornelius!"

Cornelius was afraid. He stared at the angel. "What is it, Lord?" he asked.

The angel answered, "Your prayers and gifts to poor people are like an offering to God. So he has remembered you. Now send men to Joppa. Have them bring back a man named Simon. He is also called Peter. He is staying with another Simon, a man who works with leather. His house is by the sea."

The angel who spoke to him left. Then Cornelius called two of his servants. He also called a godly soldier who was one of his attendants. He told them everything that had happened. Then he sent them to Joppa.

It was about noon the next day. The men were on their journey and were approaching the city. Peter went up on the roof to pray. He became hungry. He wanted something to eat. While the meal was being prepared, Peter had a vision. He saw heaven open up. There he saw something that looked like a large sheet. It was being let down to earth by its four corners. It had all kinds of four-footed animals in it. It also had reptiles and birds in it. Then a voice told him, "Get up, Peter. Kill and eat."

"No, Lord! I will not!" Peter replied. "I have never eaten anything that is not pure and 'clean'."

The voice spoke to him a second time. It said, "Do not say anything is not pure that God has made 'clean'."

This happened three times. Right away the sheet was taken back up to heaven.

Peter was wondering what the vision meant. At that very moment the men sent by Cornelius found Simon's house. They stopped at the gate and called out. They asked if Simon Peter was staying there.

Peter was still thinking about the vision. The Holy Spirit spoke to him. "Simon," he said, "three men are looking for you. Get up and go downstairs. Don't let anything keep you from going with them. I have sent them."

Peter went down and spoke to the men. "I'm the one you're looking for," he said. "Why have you come?"

The men replied, "We have come from Cornelius, the Roman commander. He is a good man who worships God. All the Jewish people respect him. A holy angel told him to invite you to his house. Then Cornelius can hear what you have to say." Then Peter invited the men into the house to be his guests.

The next day Peter went with the three men. Some of the believers from Joppa went along. The following day he arrived in Caesarea. Cornelius was expecting them. He had called together his relatives and close friends. When Peter entered the house, Cornelius met him. As a sign of respect, he fell at Peter's feet. But Peter made him get up. "Stand up," he said. "I am only a man myself."

As he was talking with Cornelius, Peter went inside. There he found a large group of people. He said to them, "You know that it is against our law for a Jew to enter a Gentile home. A Jew shouldn't have any close contact with a Gentile. But God has shown me that I should not say anyone is not pure and 'clean'. So when you sent for me, I came without asking any questions. May I ask why you sent for me?"

Cornelius answered, "Three days ago at this very hour I was in my house praying. It was three o'clock in the afternoon. Suddenly a man in shining clothes stood in front of me. He said, 'Cornelius, God has heard your prayer. He has remembered your gifts to poor people. Send someone to Joppa to get Simon Peter. He is a guest in the home of another Simon, who works with leather. He lives by the sea.' So I sent for you right away. It was good of you to come. Now we are all here. And God is here with us. We are ready to listen to everything the Lord has commanded you to tell us."

Then Peter began to speak. "I now realise how true it is that God treats everyone the same," he said. "He accepts people from every nation. He accepts anyone who has respect for him and does what is right. You know the message God sent to the people of Israel. It is the good news of peace through Jesus Christ. He is Lord of all. You know what has happened all through the area of Judea. It started in Galilee after John preached about baptism. You know how God anointed Jesus of Nazareth with the Holy Spirit and with power. Jesus went around doing good. He healed all who were under the devil's power. God was with him.

"We are witnesses of everything he did in the land of the Jews and in Jerusalem. They killed him by nailing him to a cross. But on the third day God raised him from the dead. God allowed Jesus to be seen. But he wasn't seen by all the people. He was seen only by us. We are witnesses whom God had already chosen. We ate and drank with him after he rose from the dead. He commanded us to preach to the people. He told us to tell people that he is the one appointed by God to judge the living and the dead. All the prophets tell about him. They say that all who believe in him have their sins forgiven through his name."

While Peter was still speaking, the Holy Spirit came on all who heard the message. Some Jewish believers had come with Peter. They were amazed because the gift of the Holy Spirit had been poured out even on

the Gentiles. They heard them speaking in languages they had not known before. They also heard them praising God.

Then Peter said, "Surely no-one can keep these people from being baptised with water. They have received the Holy Spirit just as we have." So he ordered that they be baptised in the name of Jesus Christ. Then they asked Peter to stay with them for a few days.

The apostles and the believers all through Judea heard that Gentiles had also received God's word. Peter went up to Jerusalem. There the Jewish believers found fault with him. They said, "You went into the house of Gentiles. You ate with them."

Starting from the beginning, Peter told them the whole story. "I was in the city of Joppa praying," he said. "There I had a vision. I saw something that looked like a large sheet. It was being let down from heaven by its four corners. It came down to where I

was. I looked into it and saw four-footed animals of the earth. There were also wild animals, reptiles and birds. Then I heard a voice speaking to me. 'Get up, Peter,' the voice said. 'Kill and eat.'

"I replied, 'No, Lord! I will not! Nothing that is not pure and "clean" has ever entered my mouth.'

"A second time the voice spoke from heaven. The voice said, 'Do not say anything is not pure that God has made "clean". ' This happened three times. Then the sheet was pulled up into heaven.

"Just then three men stopped at the house where I was staying. They had been sent to me from Caesarea. The Holy Spirit told me not to let anything keep me from going with them. These six brothers here went with me. We entered the man's house. He told us how he had seen an angel appear in his house. The angel said, 'Send to Joppa for Simon Peter. He has a message to bring to you. You and your whole family will be saved through it.'

"As I began to speak, the Holy Spirit came on them. He came just as he had come on us at the beginning. Then I remembered the Lord's words. 'John baptised with water,' he had said. 'But you will be baptised with the Holy Spirit.' God gave them the same gift he gave those of us who believed in the Lord Jesus Christ. So who was I to think that I could stand in God's way?"

When they heard this, they didn't object anymore. They praised God. They said, "So then, God has allowed even Gentiles to turn away from their sins. He did this so that they could live."

Some believers had been scattered by the suffering that unbelievers had caused them. They were scattered after Stephen was killed. Those believers travelled as far as Phoenicia, Cyprus and Antioch. But they spread the word only among Jews. Some believers from Cyprus

and Cyrene went to Antioch. There they began to speak to Greeks also. They told them the good news about the Lord Jesus. The Lord's power was with them. Large numbers of people believed and turned to the Lord.

The church in Jerusalem heard about this. So they sent Barnabas to Antioch. When he arrived and saw what the grace of God had done, he was glad. He told them all to remain true to the Lord with all their hearts. Barnabas was a good man. He was full of the Holy Spirit and of faith. Large numbers of people came to know the Lord.

Then Barnabas went to Tarsus to look for Saul. He

found him there. Then he brought him to Antioch. For a whole year Barnabas and Saul met with the church. They taught large numbers of people. At Antioch the believers were called Christians for the first time.

In those days some prophets came down from Jerusalem to Antioch. One of them was named Agabus. He stood up and spoke through the Spirit. He said there would not be nearly enough food anywhere in the Roman world. This happened while Claudius was the emperor. The believers decided to provide help for the brothers and sisters living in Judea. All of them helped as much as they could. They sent their gift to the elders through Barnabas and Saul.

About this time, King Herod arrested some people who belonged to the church. He planned to make them suffer greatly. He had James killed with a sword. James was John's brother. Herod saw that the death of James pleased some Jews. So he arrested Peter also. This happened during the Feast of Unleavened Bread. After Herod arrested Peter, he put him in prison. Peter was placed under guard. He was watched by four groups of four soldiers each. Herod planned to put Peter on public trial. It would take place after the Passover Feast.

So Peter was kept in prison. But the church prayed hard to God for him.

It was the night before Herod was going to bring him to trial. Peter was sleeping between two soldiers. Two chains held him there. Lookouts stood guard at the entrance. Suddenly an angel of the Lord appeared. A light shone in the prison cell. The angel struck Peter on his side. Peter woke up. "Quick!" the angel said. "Get up!" The chains fell off Peter's wrists.

Then the angel said to him, "Put on your clothes and sandals." Peter did so. "Put on your coat," the angel told him. "Follow me." Peter followed him out of the prison. But he had no idea that what the angel was doing was really happening. He thought he was seeing a vision. They passed the first and second guards. Then they came to the iron gate leading to the city. It opened for them by itself. They went through it. They walked the length of one street. Suddenly the angel left Peter.

Then Peter realised

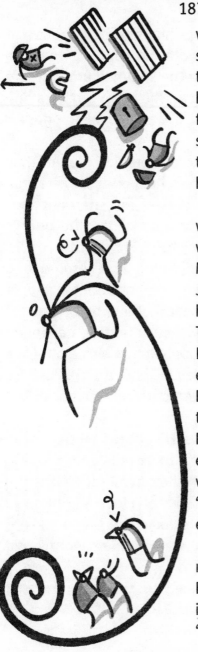

what had happened. He said, "Now I know for sure that the Lord has sent his angel. He set me free from Herod's power. He saved me from everything the Jewish people were hoping would happen."

When Peter understood what had happened, he went to Mary's house. Mary was the mother of John Mark. Many people had gathered in her home. They were praying there. Peter knocked at the outer entrance. A servant named Rhoda came to answer the door. She recognised Peter's voice. She was so excited that she ran back without opening the door. "Peter is at the door!" she exclaimed.

"You're out of your mind," they said to her. But she kept telling them it was true. So they said, "It must be his angel."

Peter kept on knocking.

When they opened the door and saw him, they were amazed. Peter motioned with his hand for them to be quiet. He explained how the Lord had brought him out of prison. "Tell James and the other brothers and sisters about this," he said. Then he went to another place.

In the morning the soldiers were bewildered. They couldn't figure out what had happened to Peter. So Herod had them look everywhere for Peter. But they didn't find him. Then Herod questioned the guards closely. He ordered that they be put to death.

Then Herod went from Judea to Caesarea and stayed there. He had been quarrelling with the people of Tyre and Sidon. So they got together and asked for a meeting with him. This was because they depended on the king's country to supply them with food. They gained the support of Blastus and then asked for peace. Blastus was a trusted personal servant of the king.

The appointed day came. Herod was seated on his throne. He was wearing his royal robes. He made a speech to the people. Then they shouted, "This is the voice of a god. It's not the voice of a man." Right away an angel of the Lord struck Herod down. Herod had not given praise to God. So he was eaten by worms and died.

But God's word continued to spread and many people believed the message.

♕ Eight ♕

Barnabas and Saul finished their task. Then they returned from Jerusalem. They took John Mark with them. In the church at Antioch there were prophets and teachers. Among them were Barnabas, Simeon, and Lucius from Cyrene. Simeon was also called Niger. Another was Manaen. He had been brought up with Herod, the ruler of Galilee. Saul was among them too. While they were worshipping the Lord and fasting, the Holy Spirit spoke. "Set apart Barnabas and Saul for me," he said. "I have appointed them to do special work." The prophets and teachers fasted and prayed. They placed their hands on Barnabas and Saul. Then they sent them off.

Barnabas and Saul were sent on their way by the Holy Spirit. They went down to Seleucia. From there they sailed to Cyprus. They arrived at Salamis. There they preached God's word in the Jewish synagogues. John was with them as their helper.

They travelled all across the island until they came to Paphos. There they met a Jew named Bar Jesus. He was an evil magician and a false prophet. He was an attendant of Sergius Paulus, the governor. Paulus was a man of understanding. He sent for Barnabas and Saul. He wanted to hear God's word. But Elymas, another evil magician, opposed them. The name Elymas means Magician. He tried to keep the governor from becoming a believer. Saul was also known as Paul. He was filled with the Holy Spirit. He looked straight at Elymas. He said to him, "You are a child of the devil! You are an enemy of everything that is right! You cheat people. You use all kinds of tricks. Won't you ever stop twisting the right ways of the Lord? Now the Lord's hand is against you. You are going to go blind. For a while you won't even be able to see the light of the sun."

Right away mist and darkness came over him. He tried to feel his way around. He wanted to find someone to lead him by the hand. When the governor saw what had happened, he believed. He was amazed at what Paul was teaching about the Lord.

From Paphos, Paul and his companions sailed to Perga in Pamphylia. There John Mark left them and returned to Jerusalem. From Perga they went on to Pisidian Antioch. On the Sabbath day they entered the synagogue and sat down. The Law and the Prophets were read aloud. Then the leaders of the synagogue sent word to Paul and his companions. They said, "Brothers, do you have any words of instruction for the people? If you do, please speak."

Paul stood up and motioned with his hand. Then he said, "Fellow Israelites, and you Gentiles who worship God, listen to me! The God of Israel chose our people who lived long ago. He blessed them greatly while

they were in Egypt. With his mighty power he led them out of that country. He put up with their behaviour for about 40 years in the desert. And he destroyed seven nations in Canaan. Then he gave the land to his people as their rightful share. All this took about 450 years.

"After this, God gave them judges until the time of Samuel the prophet. Then the people asked for a king. He gave them Saul, son of Kish. Saul was from the tribe of Benjamin. He ruled for 40 years. God removed him and made David their king. Here is God's witness about him. 'David, son of Jesse, is a man dear to my heart,' he said. 'David will do everything I want him to do.'

"From this man's family line God has brought to Israel the Saviour Jesus. This is what he had promised. Before Jesus came, John preached that we should turn away from our sins and be baptised. He preached this to all Israel. John was coming to the end of his work. 'Who do you suppose I am?' he said. 'I am not the one you are looking for. But there is someone coming after me. I am not good enough to untie his sandals.'

"Listen, fellow children of Abraham! Listen, you Gentiles who worship God! This message of salvation has been sent to us. The people of Jerusalem and their rulers did not recognise Jesus. By finding him guilty, they made the prophets' words come true. These are read every Sabbath day. The people and their rulers had no reason at all for sentencing Jesus to death. But they asked Pilate to have him killed. They did everything that had been written about Jesus. Then they took him down from the cross. They laid him in a tomb. But God raised him from the dead. For many days he was seen

by those who had travelled with him from Galilee to Jerusalem. Now they are telling our people about Jesus.

"We are telling you the good news. What God promised our people long ago he has done for us, their children. He has raised up Jesus. This is what is written in the second Psalm. It says,

> "'You are my son.
>   Today I have become your father.' *(from Psalm 2)*

God raised Jesus from the dead. He will never rot in the grave. As God has said,

> "'Holy and sure blessings were promised
>   to David.
>   I will give them to you.'   *(from the prophet Isaiah)*

In another place it also says,

> "'You will not let your holy one rot away.'
> *(from Psalm 16)*

"David carried out God's purpose while he lived. Then he died. He was buried with his people. His body rotted away. But the one whom God raised from the dead did not rot away.

"My friends, here is what I want you to know. I announce to you that your sins can be forgiven because of what Jesus has done. Through him everyone who believes is set free from every sin. Moses' law could not make you right in God's eyes. Be careful! Don't let what the prophets spoke about happen to you. They said,

> "'Look, you who make fun of the truth!
>   Wonder and die!

> I am going to do something in your days
> 　　that you would never believe.
> You wouldn't believe it even if someone
> 　　told you.'"　　*(from the prophet Habakkuk)*

Paul and Barnabas started to leave the synagogue. The people invited them to say more about these things on the next Sabbath day. The people were told they could leave the service. Many Jews followed Paul and Barnabas. Many Gentiles who faithfully worshipped the God of the Jews did the same. Paul and Barnabas talked with them. They tried to get them to keep living in God's grace.

On the next Sabbath day, almost the whole city gathered. They gathered to hear the word of the Lord. When the Jews saw the crowds, they became very jealous. They began to disagree with what Paul was saying. They said evil things against him.

Then Paul and Barnabas answered them boldly. "We had to speak God's word to you first," they said. "But you don't accept it. You don't think you are good enough for eternal life. So now we are turning to the Gentiles. This is what the Lord has commanded us to do. He said,

> "'I have made you a light for the Gentiles.
> 　　You will bring salvation to the whole earth.'"
> *(from the prophet Isaiah)*

When the Gentiles heard this, they were glad. They honoured the word of the Lord. All who were appointed for eternal life believed.

The word of the Lord spread through the whole area. But the Jewish leaders stirred up the important women who worshipped God. They also stirred up the men who were leaders in the city. The Jewish leaders tried to get the women and men to attack Paul and Barnabas. They threw Paul and Barnabas out of that area. Paul and Barnabas shook the dust off their feet. This was a warning to the people who had opposed them. Then Paul and Barnabas went on to Iconium. The believers were filled with joy and with the Holy Spirit.

At Iconium, Paul and Barnabas went into the Jewish synagogue as usual. They spoke there with great power. Large numbers of Jews and Greeks became believers. But the Jews who refused to believe stirred up some of the Gentiles who were there. They turned them against the two men and the new believers. So Paul and Barnabas spent a lot of time there. They spoke boldly for the Lord. He gave them the ability to do signs and wonders. In this way the Lord showed that they were telling the truth about his grace. The people of the city did not agree with one another. Some were on the side of the Jews. Others were on the side of the apostles. Jews and Gentiles alike planned to treat Paul and Barnabas badly. Their leaders agreed. They planned to kill them by throwing stones at them. But Paul and Barnabas found out about the plan. They escaped to the Lycaonian cities of Lystra and Derbe and to the surrounding area. There they continued to preach the good news.

In Lystra there sat a man who couldn't walk. He hadn't been able to use his feet since the day he was born. He listened as Paul spoke. Paul looked right at him. He saw that the man had faith to be healed. So he called out, "Stand up on your feet!" Then the man jumped up and began to walk.

The crowd saw what Paul had done. They shouted in the Lycaonian language. "The gods have come down to us in human form!" they exclaimed. They called Barnabas Zeus. Paul was the main speaker. So they called him Hermes. Just outside the city was the temple of the god Zeus. The priest of Zeus brought

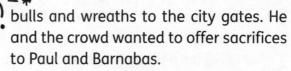

bulls and wreaths to the city gates. He and the crowd wanted to offer sacrifices to Paul and Barnabas.

But the apostles Barnabas and Paul heard about this. So they tore their clothes. They rushed out into the crowd. They shouted, "Friends, why are you doing this? We are only human, just like you. We are bringing you good news. Turn away from these worthless things. Turn to the living God. He is the one who made the heavens and the earth and the sea. He made everything in them. In the past, he let all nations go their own way. But he has given proof of what he is like. He has shown kindness by giving you rain from heaven. He gives you crops in their seasons. He provides you with plenty of food. He fills your hearts with joy." Paul and Barnabas told them all these things. But they had trouble keeping the crowd from offering sacrifices to them.

Then some Jews came from Antioch and Iconium. They won the crowd over to their side. They threw stones at Paul. They thought he was dead, so they dragged him out of the city. The believers gathered around Paul. Then he got up and went back into the city. The next day he and Barnabas left for Derbe.

Paul and Barnabas preached the good news in the city of Derbe. They won large numbers of followers. Then they returned to Lystra, Iconium and Antioch. There they helped the believers gain strength. They told them to remain faithful to what they had been taught. "We must go through many hard times to enter God's kingdom," they said. Paul and Barnabas appointed elders for them in each church. The elders had trusted in the Lord. Paul and Barnabas prayed and fasted. They placed the elders in the Lord's care. After going through Pisidia, Paul and Barnabas came into Pamphylia. They preached the good news in Perga. Then they went down to Attalia.

From Attalia they sailed back to Antioch. In Antioch they had been put in God's care to preach the good news. They had now completed the work God had given them to do. When they arrived at Antioch, they gathered the church together. They reported all that God had done through them. They told how he had opened a way for the Gentiles to believe. And they stayed there a long time with the believers.

Certain people came down from Judea to Antioch. Here is what they were teaching the believers. "Moses commanded you to be circumcised," they said. "If you aren't, you can't be saved." But Paul and Barnabas didn't agree with this. They argued strongly with them. So Paul and Barnabas were appointed to go up to Jerusalem. Some other believers were chosen to go with them. They were told to ask the apostles and elders about this question. The church sent them on their way. They travelled through Phoenicia and Samaria. There they told how the Gentiles had turned to God. This news made all the believers very glad. When they arrived in Jerusalem, the church welcomed them. The apostles and elders welcomed them too. Then Paul and Barnabas reported everything God had done through them.

Some of the believers were Pharisees. They stood up and said, "The Gentiles must be circumcised. They must obey the law of Moses."

The apostles and elders met to consider this question. After they had talked it over, Peter got up and spoke to them. "Brothers," he said, "you know that some time ago God chose me. He appointed me to take the good news to the Gentiles. He wanted them to hear the good news and believe. God knows the human heart. By giving the Holy Spirit to the Gentiles, he showed that he accepted them. He did the same for them as he had done for us. God showed that there is no difference between us and them. That's because he made their hearts pure because of their faith. Now then, why are you trying to test God? You test him when you put a heavy load on the shoulders of Gentiles. Our people of long ago couldn't carry that load. We can't either. No! We believe we are saved through the grace of our Lord Jesus. The Gentiles are saved in the same way."

Everyone became quiet as they listened to Barnabas and Paul. They were telling about the signs and wonders God had done through them among the Gentiles. When they finished, James spoke up. "Brothers," he said, "listen to me. Simon Peter has explained to us what God has now done. He has chosen some of the Gentiles to be among his very own people. The prophets' words agree with that. They say,

> " 'After this I will return
>> and set up again David's fallen tent.
> I will rebuild what was destroyed.
>> I will make it what it used to be.
> Then everyone else can look to the Lord.
>> This includes all the Gentiles who belong to
>> me, says the Lord.
> The Lord is the one who does these things.'

(from the prophet Amos)

The Lord does things that have been known from long ago.

"Now here is my decision. We should not make it hard for the Gentiles who are turning to God. Here is what we should write to them. They must not eat food that has been made impure by being offered to statues of gods.

They must not commit sexual sins. They must not eat the meat of animals that have been choked to death. And they must not drink blood. These laws of Moses have been preached in every city from the earliest times. They are read out loud in the synagogues every Sabbath day."

Then the apostles, the elders and the whole church decided what to do. They would choose some of their own men who were leaders among the believers. They would send them to Antioch with Paul and Barnabas. So they chose Judas Barsabbas and Silas. They were leaders among the believers. Here is the letter they sent with them.

The apostles and elders, your brothers, are writing this letter.

We are sending it to the Gentile believers in Antioch, Syria and Cilicia.

Greetings.

We have heard that some of our people came

to you and caused trouble. You were upset by what they said. But we had given them no authority to go. So we all agreed to send our dear friends Barnabas and Paul to you. We chose some other men to go with them. Barnabas and Paul have put their lives in danger. They did it for the name of our Lord Jesus Christ. So we are sending Judas and Silas with them. What they say will agree with this letter. Here is what seemed good to the Holy Spirit and to us. We will not give you a load that is too heavy. So here are a few basic rules. Don't eat food that has been offered to statues of gods. Don't drink blood. Don't eat the meat of animals that have been choked to death. And don't commit sexual sins. You will do well to keep away from these things.

Farewell.

So the men were sent down to Antioch. There they gathered the church together. They gave the letter to them. The people read it. They were glad for its message of hope. Judas and Silas were prophets. They

said many things to give strength and hope to the believers. Judas and Silas stayed there for some time. Then the believers sent them away with the blessing of peace. They sent them back to those who had sent them out. Paul and Barnabas remained in Antioch. There they and many others taught and preached the word of the Lord.

Some time later Paul spoke to Barnabas. "Let's go back to all the towns where we preached the word of the Lord," he said. "Let's visit the believers and see how they are doing." Barnabas wanted to take John Mark with them. But Paul didn't think it was wise to take him. Mark had deserted them in Pamphylia. He hadn't continued with them in their work. Barnabas and Paul strongly disagreed with each other. So they went their separate ways. Barnabas took Mark and sailed for Cyprus. But Paul chose Silas. The believers asked the Lord to give his grace to Paul and Silas as they went.

Paul travelled through Syria and Cilicia. He gave strength to the churches there.

Paul came to Derbe. Then he went on to Lystra. A believer named Timothy lived there. His mother was Jewish and a believer. His father was a Greek.

The believers at Lystra and Iconium said good things about Timothy. Paul wanted to take him along on the journey. So he circumcised Timothy because of the Jews who lived in that area. They all knew that Timothy's father was a Greek. Paul and his companions travelled from town to town. They reported what the apostles and elders in Jerusalem had decided. The people were supposed to obey what was in the report. So the churches were made strong in the faith. The number of believers grew every day.

♕ Nine ♕

Paul and his companions travelled all through the area of Phrygia and Galatia. The Holy Spirit had kept them from preaching the word in Asia Minor. They came to the border of Mysia. From there they tried to enter Bithynia. But the Spirit of Jesus would not let them. So they passed by Mysia. Then they went down to Troas. During the night Paul had a vision. He saw a man from Macedonia standing and begging him. "Come over to Macedonia!" the man said. "Help us!" After Paul had seen the vision, we got ready at once to leave for Macedonia. We decided that God had called us to preach the good news there.

At Troas we got into a boat. We sailed straight for Samothrace. The next day we went on to Neapolis. From there we travelled to Philippi, a Roman colony. It is an important city in that part of Macedonia. We stayed there several days.

On the Sabbath day we went outside the city gate. We walked down to the river. There we expected to find a place of prayer. We sat down and began to speak to the women who had gathered together. One of the women listening was from the city of Thyatira. Her name was Lydia, and her business was selling purple cloth. She was a worshipper of God. The Lord opened her heart to accept Paul's message. She and her family were baptised. Then she invited us to her home. "Do you consider me a believer in the Lord?" she asked. "If you do, come and stay at my house." She succeeded in getting us to go home with her.

One day we were going to the place of prayer. On the way we were met by a female slave. She had a spirit that helped her tell people what was going to happen. She earned a lot of money for her owners by doing this. She followed Paul and the rest of us around. She shouted, "These men serve the Most High God. They are telling you how to be saved." She kept this up for many days. Finally Paul became upset. Turning around, he spoke to the spirit that was in her. "In the name of Jesus Christ," he said, "I command you to come out of her!" At that very moment the spirit left the woman.

Her owners realised that their hope of making money was gone. So they grabbed Paul and Silas. They dragged them into the market place

to face the authorities. They brought them to the judges. "These men are Jews," her owners said. "They are making trouble in our city. They are suggesting practices that are against Roman law. These are practices we can't accept or take part in."

The crowd joined the attack against Paul and Silas. The judges ordered that Paul and Silas be stripped and beaten with rods. They were whipped without mercy. Then they were thrown into prison. The jailer was commanded to guard them carefully. When he received these orders, he put Paul and Silas deep inside the prison. He fastened their feet so they couldn't get away.

About midnight Paul and Silas were praying. They were also singing hymns to God. The other prisoners were listening to them. Suddenly there was a powerful earthquake. It shook the prison from top to bottom. All at once the prison doors flew open. Everyone's chains came loose. The jailer woke up. He saw that the prison doors were open. He pulled out his sword and was going to kill himself. He thought the prisoners had escaped. "Don't harm yourself!" Paul shouted. "We are all here!"

The jailer called out for some lights. He rushed in, shaking with fear. He fell down in front of Paul and Silas. Then he brought them out. He asked, "Sirs, what must I do to be saved?"

They replied, "Believe in the Lord Jesus. Then you and everyone living in your house will be saved." They spoke the word of the Lord to him. They also spoke to all the others in his house. At that hour of the night, the jailer took Paul and Silas and washed their wounds. Right away he and everyone who lived with him were baptised. The jailer brought them into his house. He set a meal in front of them. He and everyone who lived with him were filled with joy. They had become believers in God.

Early in the morning the judges sent their officers to the jailer. They ordered him, "Let those men go." The jailer told Paul, "The judges have ordered me to set you and Silas free. You can leave now. Go in peace."

But Paul replied to the officers. "They beat us in public," he said. "We weren't given a trial. And we are Roman citizens! They threw us into prison. And now do they want to get rid of us quietly? No! Let them come themselves and personally lead us out."

The officers reported this to the judges. When the judges heard that Paul and Silas were Roman citizens, they became afraid. So they came and said they were sorry. They led them out of the prison. Then they asked them to leave the city. After Paul and Silas came out of the prison, they went to Lydia's house. There they met with the brothers and sisters. They told them to be brave. Then they left.

Paul and those travelling with him passed through Amphipolis and Apollonia. They came to Thessalonica. A Jewish synagogue was there. Paul went into the synagogue as he usually did. For three Sabbath days in a row he talked with the Jews about the Scriptures. He explained and proved that the Messiah had to suffer and rise from the dead. "This Jesus I am telling you about is the Messiah!" he said. His words won over some of the Jews. They joined Paul and Silas. A large number of Greeks who worshipped God joined them too. So did quite a few important women.

But other Jews were jealous. So they rounded up some evil people from the market place. Forming a crowd, they started all kinds of trouble in the city. The Jews rushed to Jason's house. They were looking for Paul and Silas. They wanted to bring them out to the crowd. But they couldn't find them. So they dragged Jason and some other believers to the city officials. "These men have caused trouble all over the world," they shouted. "Now they have come here. Jason has welcomed them into his house. They are all disobeying Caesar's commands. They say there is another king. He is called Jesus." When the crowd and the city officials heard this, they became very upset. They made Jason and the others give them money. The officials did this to make sure they would return to the court. Then they let Jason and the others go.

As soon as it was night, the believers sent Paul and Silas away to Berea. When they arrived, they went to the Jewish synagogue. The Berean Jews were very glad to receive Paul's message. They studied the Scriptures carefully

every day. They wanted to see if what Paul said was true. So they were more noble than the Thessalonian Jews. Because of this, many of the Berean Jews believed. A number of important Greek women also became believers. And so did many Greek men.

But the Jews in Thessalonica found out that Paul was preaching God's word in Berea. So some of them went there too. They stirred up the crowds and got them all worked up. Right away the believers sent Paul to the coast. But Silas and Timothy stayed in Berea. The believers who went with Paul took him to Athens. Then they returned with orders that Silas and Timothy were supposed to join him as soon as they could.

Paul was waiting for Silas and Timothy in Athens. He was very upset to see that the city was full of statues of gods. So he went to the synagogue. There he talked both with Jews and with Greeks who worshipped God. Each day he spoke with anyone who happened to be in the market place. A group of Epicurean and Stoic thinkers began to argue with him. Some of them asked, "What is this fellow chattering about?" Others said, "He seems to be telling us about gods we've never heard of." They said this because Paul was preaching the good news about Jesus. He was telling them that Jesus had risen from the dead. They took him to a meeting of the Areopagus. There they said to him, "What is this new teaching you're giving us? You have some strange ideas we've never heard before. We would like to know what they mean." All the people of

Athens spent their time talking about and listening to the latest ideas. People from other lands who lived there did the same.

Then Paul stood up in the meeting of the Areopagus. He said, "People of Athens! I see that you are very religious in every way. As I walked around, I looked carefully at the things you worship. I even found an altar with

TO AN UNKNOWN GOD

written on it. So you don't know what you are worshipping. Now I am going to tell you about this 'unknown god'.

"He is the God who made the world. He also made everything in it. He is the Lord of heaven and earth. He doesn't live in temples built by human hands. He is not served by human hands. He doesn't need anything. Instead, he himself gives life and breath to all people. He also gives them everything else they have. From one man he made all the people of the world. Now they live all over the earth. He decided exactly when they should live. And he decided exactly where they should live. God did this so that people would seek him. And perhaps they would reach out for him and find him. They would find him even though he is not far from any of us. 'In him we live and move and exist.' As some of your own poets have also said, 'We are his children.'

"Yes, we are God's children. So we shouldn't think that God is made out of gold or silver or stone. He isn't a statue planned and made by clever people. In the past, God didn't judge people for what they didn't know. But now he commands all people everywhere to turn away from their sins. He has set a day when he will judge the world fairly. He has appointed a man to be its judge. God has proved this to everyone by raising that man from the dead."

They heard Paul talk about the dead being raised. Some of them made fun of this idea. But others said, "We want to hear you speak about this again." So Paul left the meeting of the Areopagus. Some of the people became followers of Paul and believed in Jesus. Dionysius was one of them. He was a member of the

Areopagus. A woman named Damaris also became a believer. And so did some others.

After this, Paul left Athens and went to Corinth. There he met a Jew named Aquila, who was a native of Pontus. Aquila had recently come from Italy with his wife Priscilla. The emperor Claudius had ordered all Jews to leave Rome. Paul went to see Aquila and Priscilla. They were tentmakers, just as he was. So he stayed and worked with them. Every Sabbath day he went to the synagogue. He was trying to get both Jews and Greeks to believe in the Lord.

Silas and Timothy came from Macedonia. Then Paul spent all his time preaching. He was a witness to the Jews that Jesus was the Messiah. But they opposed Paul. They treated him badly. So he shook out his clothes in protest. Then he said to them, "God's judgment against you will be your own fault! Don't blame me for it! From now on I will go to the Gentiles."

Then Paul left the synagogue and went to the house next door. It was the house of Titius Justus, a man who worshipped God. Crispus was the synagogue leader. He and everyone living in his house came to believe in the Lord. Many others who lived in Corinth heard Paul. They too believed and were baptised.

One night the Lord spoke to Paul in a vision. "Don't be afraid," he said. "Keep on speaking. Don't be silent.

I am with you. No-one will attack you and harm you. I have many people in this city." So Paul stayed in Corinth for a year and a half. He taught them God's word.

At that time Gallio was governor of Achaia. The Jews of Corinth got together and attacked Paul. They brought him into court. They made a charge against Paul. They said, "This man is talking people into worshipping God in wrong ways. Those ways are against the law."

Paul was about to give reasons for his actions. But just then Gallio spoke to them. He said, "You Jews don't claim that Paul has committed a great or small crime. If you did, it would make sense for me to listen to you. But this is about your own law. It is a question of words and names. Settle the matter yourselves. I will not be a judge of such things." So he made them leave. Then the crowd there turned against Sosthenes, the synagogue leader. They beat him up in front of the governor. But Gallio didn't care at all.

Paul stayed in Corinth for some time. Then he left the brothers and sisters and sailed for Syria. Priscilla and Aquila went with him. Before he sailed, he had his hair cut off at Cenchreae. He did this because he had made a promise to God. They arrived at Ephesus. There Paul said goodbye to Priscilla and Aquila. He himself went into the synagogue and talked with the Jews. The Jews asked him to spend more time with them. But he said no. As he left, he made them a promise. "If God wants me to," he said, "I will come back." Then he sailed from Ephesus. When he landed at Caesarea, he went up to Jerusalem. There he greeted the church. He then went down to Antioch.

Paul spent some time in Antioch. Then he left and travelled all over Galatia and Phrygia. He gave strength to all the believers there.

At that time a Jew named Apollos came to Ephesus. He was an educated man from Alexandria. He knew the Scriptures very well. Apollos had been taught the way of the Lord. He spoke with great power. He taught the truth about Jesus. But he only knew about John's baptism. He began to speak boldly in the synagogue. Priscilla and Aquila heard him. So they invited him to their home. There they gave him a better understanding of the way of God.

Apollos wanted to go to Achaia. The brothers and sisters agreed with him. They wrote to the believers there. They asked them to welcome him. When he arrived, he was a great help to those who had become believers by God's grace. In public meetings, he argued strongly against Jews who disagreed with him. He proved from the Scriptures that Jesus was the Messiah.

While Apollos was at Corinth, Paul took the road to Ephesus. When he arrived, he found some believers there. He asked them, "Did you receive the Holy Spirit when you became believers?"

"No," they answered. "We haven't even heard that there is a Holy Spirit."

So Paul asked, "Then what baptism did you receive?"

"John's baptism," they replied.

Paul said, "John baptised people, calling them to turn away from their sins. He told them to believe in the one who was coming after him. Jesus is that one." After hearing this, they were baptised in the name of the Lord Jesus. Paul placed his hands on them. Then the Holy Spirit came on them. They spoke in languages they had not known before. They also prophesied. There were about 12 men in all.

Paul entered the synagogue. There he spoke boldly for three months. He gave good reasons for believing the truth about God's kingdom. But some of them wouldn't listen. They refused to believe. In public they said evil things about the Way of Jesus. So Paul left them. He took the believers with him. Each day he talked with people in the lecture hall of Tyrannus. This went on for two years. So all the Jews and Greeks who lived in Asia Minor heard the word of the Lord.

God did amazing miracles through Paul. Even handkerchiefs and aprons that had touched him were taken to those who were ill. When this happened, their diseases were healed and evil spirits left them.

Some Jews went around driving out evil spirits. They tried to use the name of the Lord Jesus to set free those who were controlled by demons. They said, "In Jesus' name I command you to come out. He is the Jesus that Paul is preaching about." Seven sons of Sceva were doing this. Sceva was a Jewish chief priest. One day the evil spirit answered them, "I know Jesus.

And I know about Paul. But who are you?" Then the man who had the evil spirit jumped on Sceva's sons. He overpowered them all. He gave them a terrible beating. They ran out of the house naked and bleeding.

The Jews and Greeks living in Ephesus heard about this. They were all overcome with fear. They held the name of the Lord Jesus in high honour. Many who believed now came and openly admitted what they had done. A number of those who had practised evil magic brought their scrolls together. They set them on fire out in the open. They added up the value of the scrolls. The scrolls were worth more than someone could earn in two lifetimes. The word of the Lord spread everywhere. It became more and more powerful.

♔ Ten ♔

After all this had happened, Paul decided to go to Jerusalem. He went through Macedonia and Achaia. "After I have been to Jerusalem," he said, "I must visit Rome also." He sent Timothy and Erastus, two of his helpers, to Macedonia. But he stayed a little longer in Asia Minor.

At that time many people became very upset about the Way of Jesus. There was a man named Demetrius who made things out of silver. He made silver models of the temple of the goddess Artemis. He brought in a lot of business for the other skilled workers there. One day he called them together. He also called others who were in the same kind of business. "My friends," he said, "you know that we make good money from our work. You have seen and heard what this fellow Paul is doing. He has talked to large numbers of people here in Ephesus. Almost everywhere in Asia Minor he has led people away from our gods. He says that the gods made by human hands are not gods at all. Our work is in danger of losing its good name. People's faith in the temple of the great goddess Artemis will be weakened. Now she is worshipped all over Asia Minor and the whole world. But soon she will be robbed of her greatness."

When they heard this, they became very angry. They began shouting, "Great is Artemis of the Ephesians!" Soon people were making trouble in the whole city. They all rushed into the theatre. They dragged Gaius and Aristarchus along with them. These two men had come with Paul from Macedonia. Paul wanted to appear in front of the crowd. But the believers wouldn't let him. Some of the officials in Asia Minor were friends of Paul. They sent him a message, begging him not to go into the theatre.

The crowd didn't know what was going on. Some were shouting one thing and some another. Most of the people didn't even know why they were there. The Jews in the crowd pushed Alexander to the front. They tried to tell him what to say. But he motioned for them to be quiet. He was about to give the people reasons for his actions. But then they realised that he was a Jew. So they all shouted the same thing for about two hours. "Great is Artemis of the Ephesians!" they yelled.

The city clerk quietened the crowd down. "People of Ephesus!" he said. "The city of Ephesus guards the temple of the great Artemis. The whole world knows this. They know that Ephesus guards her statue, which fell from heaven. These facts can't be questioned. So calm down. Don't do anything foolish. These men haven't robbed any temples. They haven't said evil things against our female god. But you have brought them here anyhow. Demetrius and the other skilled workers may feel they have been wronged by someone. Let them bring charges. The courts are open. We have our governors. Is there anything else you want to bring up? Settle it in a court of law. As it is, we are in danger of being charged with a crime. We could be charged with causing all this trouble today. There is no reason for it. So we wouldn't be able to explain what has happened." After he said this, he sent the people away.

All the trouble came to an end. Then Paul sent for the believers. After encouraging them, he said goodbye. He then left for Macedonia. He travelled through that area, speaking many words of hope to the people. Finally he arrived in Greece. There he stayed for three months. He was just about to sail for Syria. But some Jews were making plans against him. So he decided to go back through Macedonia. Sopater, son of Pyrrhus, from Berea went with him. Aristarchus and Secundus from Thessalonica, Gaius from Derbe, and Timothy went too. Tychicus and Trophimus from Asia Minor also went with him. These men went on ahead. They waited for us at Troas. But we sailed from Philippi after the Feast of Unleavened Bread. Five days later we joined the others at Troas. We stayed there for seven days.

On the first day of the week we met to break bread and eat together. Paul spoke to the people. He kept on talking until midnight because he planned to leave the next day. There were many lamps in the room upstairs where we were meeting. A young man named Eutychus was sitting in a window. He sank into a deep sleep as Paul talked on and on. Sound asleep, Eutychus fell from the third floor. When they picked him up from the ground, he was dead. Paul went down and threw himself on the young man. He put his arms around

him. "Don't be alarmed," he told them. "He's alive!" Then Paul went upstairs again. He broke bread and ate with them. He kept on talking until daylight. Then he left. The people took the young man home. They were greatly comforted because he was alive.

We went on ahead to the ship. We sailed for Assos. There we were going to take Paul on board. He had planned it this way because he wanted to go to Assos by land. So he met us there. We took him on board and went on to Mitylene. The next day we sailed from there. We arrived near Chios. The day after that we crossed over to Samos. We arrived at Miletus the next day. Paul had decided to sail past Ephesus. He didn't want to spend time in Asia Minor. He was in a hurry to get to Jerusalem. If he could, he wanted to be there by the day of Pentecost.

From Miletus, Paul sent for the elders of the church at Ephesus. When they arrived, he spoke to them. "You know how I lived the whole time I was with you," he said. "From the first day I came into Asia Minor, I served the Lord with tears and without pride. I served him when I was greatly tested. I was tested by the evil plans of the Jews who disagreed with me. You know that nothing has kept me from preaching whatever would help you. I have taught you in public and from house to house. I have told both Jews and Greeks that they must turn away from their sins to God. They must have faith in our Lord Jesus.

"Now I am going to Jerusalem. The Holy Spirit

compels me. I don't know what will happen to me there. I only know that in every city the Spirit warns me. He tells me that I will face prison and suffering. But my life means nothing to me. My only goal is to finish the race. I want to complete the work the Lord Jesus has given me. He wants me to tell others about the good news of God's grace.

"I have spent time with you preaching about the kingdom. I know that none of you will ever see me again. So I tell you today that I am not guilty if any of you don't believe. I haven't let anyone keep me from telling you everything God wants you to do. Keep watch over yourselves. Keep watch over all the believers. The Holy Spirit has made you leaders over them. Be shepherds of God's church. He bought it with his own blood. I know that after I leave, wild wolves will come in among you. They won't spare any of the sheep. Even men from your own people will rise up and twist the truth. They want to get the believers to follow them. So be on your guard! Remember that for three years I never stopped warning you. Night and day I warned each of you with tears.

"Now I trust God to take care of you. I commit you to the message about his grace. It can build you up. Then you will share in what God plans to give all his people. I haven't longed for anyone's silver or gold or clothing. You yourselves know that I have used my own hands to meet my needs. I have also met the needs of my companions. In everything I did, I showed you that we must work hard and help the weak. We must remember the words of the Lord Jesus. He said, 'It is more blessed to give than to receive.'"

Paul finished speaking. Then he got down on his knees with all of them and prayed. They all wept as they hugged and kissed him. Paul had said that they would never see him again. That's what hurt them the most. Then they went with him to the ship.

After we had torn ourselves away from the Ephesian elders, we headed out to sea. We sailed straight to Kos. The next day we went to Rhodes. From there we continued on to Patara. We found a ship crossing over to Phoenicia. So we went on board and headed out to sea. We came near Cyprus and passed to the south of it. Then we sailed on to Syria. We landed at Tyre. There our ship was supposed to unload. We looked for the believers there and stayed with them for seven days. The believers tried to keep Paul from going on to Jerusalem. They were led by the Holy Spirit to do this. When it was time to leave, we continued on our way. All the believers, including their whole families, went with us out of the city. There on the beach we got down on our knees to

pray. We said goodbye to each other. Then we went on board the ship. And they returned home.

Continuing on from Tyre, we landed at Ptolemais. There we greeted the brothers and sisters. We stayed with them for a day. The next day we left and arrived at Caesarea. We stayed at the house of Philip the evangelist. He was one of the seven deacons. He had four unmarried daughters who prophesied.

We stayed there several days. Then a prophet named Agabus came down from Judea. He came over to us. Then he took Paul's belt and tied his own hands and feet with it. He said, "The Holy Spirit says, 'This is how the Jewish leaders in Jerusalem will tie up the owner of this belt. They will hand him over to the Gentiles.'"

When we heard this, we all begged Paul not to go up to Jerusalem. He asked, "Why are you crying? Why are you breaking my heart? I'm ready to be put in prison. In fact, I'm ready to die in Jerusalem for the Lord Jesus." We couldn't change his mind. So we gave up. We said, "May what the Lord wants to happen be done."

After this, we started on our way to Jerusalem. Some of the believers from Caesarea went with us. They brought us to Mnason's home. We were supposed to stay there. Mnason was from Cyprus. He was one of the first believers.

When we arrived in Jerusalem, the brothers and sisters gave us a warm welcome. The next day Paul and the rest of us went to see James. All the elders were there.

Paul greeted them. Then he reported everything God had done among the Gentiles through his work.

When they heard this, they praised God. Then they spoke to Paul. "Brother," they said, "you see that thousands of Jews have become believers. All of them try very hard to obey the law. They have been told that you teach Jews to turn away from the Law of Moses. You teach this to the Jews who live among the Gentiles. They think that you teach those Jews not to circumcise their children. They think that you teach them to give up our Jewish ways. What should we do? They will certainly hear that you have come. So do what we tell you. There are four men with us who have made a promise to God. Take them with you. Join them in the Jewish practice that makes people pure and 'clean'. Pay their expenses so they can have their heads shaved. Then everyone will know that these reports about you are not true in any way. They will know that you yourself obey the law. We have already given written directions to the believers who are not Jews. They must not eat food that has been offered to statues of gods. They must not drink blood. They must not eat the meat of animals that have been choked to death. And they must not commit sexual sins."

The next day Paul took the men with him. They all made themselves pure and "clean" in the usual way. Then Paul went to the temple. There he reported the date when the days of cleansing would end. At that time the proper offering would be made for each of them.

The seven days of cleansing were almost over. Some Jews from Asia Minor saw Paul at the temple. They stirred up the whole crowd and grabbed Paul. "Fellow Israelites, help us!" they shouted. "This is the man who teaches everyone in all places against our people. He speaks against our law and against this holy place. Besides, he has brought Greeks into the temple. He has made this holy place 'unclean'." They said this because they had seen Trophimus the Ephesian in the city with Paul. They thought Paul had brought him into the temple.

The whole city was stirred up. People came running from all directions. They grabbed Paul and dragged him out of the temple. Right away the temple gates were shut. The people were trying to kill Paul. But news reached the commander of the Roman troops. He heard that people were making trouble in the whole city of Jerusalem. Right away he took some officers and soldiers with him. They ran down to the crowd. The people causing the trouble saw the commander and his soldiers. So they stopped beating Paul.

The commander came up and arrested Paul. He ordered him to be held with two chains. Then he asked who Paul was and what he had done. Some in the crowd shouted one thing, some another. But the commander couldn't get the facts because of all the noise. So he ordered that Paul be taken into the fort. Paul reached the steps. But then the mob became so wild that he had to be carried by the soldiers. The crowd that followed kept shouting, "Get rid of him!"

The soldiers were about to take Paul into the fort. Then he asked the commander, "May I say something to you?"

"Do you speak Greek?" he replied. "Aren't you the Egyptian who turned some of our people against their leaders? Didn't you lead 4,000 terrorists out into the desert some time ago?"

Paul answered, "I am a Jew from Tarsus in Cilicia. I am a citizen of an important city. Please let me speak to the people."

The commander told him he could. So Paul stood on the steps and motioned to the crowd. When all of them were quiet, he spoke to them in the Aramaic language. "Brothers and fathers," Paul began, "listen to me now. I want to give you reasons for my actions."

When they heard that he was speaking to them in Aramaic, they became very quiet.

Then Paul said, "I am a Jew. I was born in Tarsus in Cilicia, but I grew up here in Jerusalem. I studied with Gamaliel. I was well trained by him in the law given to our people long ago. I wanted to serve God as much as any of you do today. I hurt the followers of the Way of Jesus. I sent many of them to their death. I arrested men and women. I threw them into prison. The high priest and the whole Council can be witnesses of this themselves. I even had some official letters they had written to their friends in Damascus. So I went there to bring these people as prisoners to Jerusalem to be punished.

"I had almost reached Damascus. About noon a

bright light from heaven suddenly flashed around me. I fell to the ground and heard a voice speak to me. 'Saul! Saul!' it said. 'Why are you opposing me?'

"'Who are you, Lord?' I asked.

"'I am Jesus of Nazareth,' he replied. 'I am the one you are opposing.' The light was seen by my companions. But they didn't understand the voice of the one speaking to me.

"'What should I do, Lord?' I asked.

"'Get up,' the Lord said. 'Go into Damascus. There you will be told everything you have been given to do.' The brightness of the light had blinded me. So my companions led me by the hand into Damascus.

"A man named Ananias came to see me. He was

a godly Jew who obeyed the law. All the Jews living there respected him very much. He stood beside me and said, 'Brother Saul, receive your sight!' At that very moment I was able to see him.

"Then he said, 'The God of our people has chosen you. He wanted to tell you his plans for you. You have seen the Blameless One. You have heard words from his mouth. Now you will tell everyone about what you have seen and heard. So what are you waiting for? Get up and call on his name. Be baptised. Have your sins washed away.'

"I returned to Jerusalem and was praying at the temple. Then it seemed to me that I was dreaming. I saw the Lord speaking to me. 'Quick!' he said. 'Leave Jerusalem at once. The people here will not accept what you tell them about me.'

"'Lord,' I replied, 'these people know what I used to do. I went from one synagogue to another and put believers in prison. I also beat them. Stephen was a man who told other people about you. I stood there when he was killed. I had agreed that he should die. I even guarded the coats of those who were killing him.'

"Then the Lord said to me, 'Go. I will send you far away to people who are not Jews.'"

The crowd listened to Paul until he said this. Then they shouted, "Kill him! He isn't fit to live!"

They shouted and threw off their coats. They threw dust into the air. So the commanding officer ordered that Paul be taken into the fort. He gave orders for Paul to be whipped and questioned. He wanted to find out why the people were shouting at him like this. A commander was standing there as they stretched Paul out to be whipped. Paul said to him, "Does the law allow you to whip a Roman citizen who hasn't even been found guilty?"

When the commander heard this, he went to the commanding officer and reported it. "What are you going to do?" the commander asked. "This man is a Roman citizen."

So the commanding officer went to Paul. "Tell me," he asked. "Are you a Roman citizen?"

"Yes, I am," Paul answered.

Then the officer said, "I had to pay a lot of money to become a citizen."

"But I was born a citizen," Paul replied.

Right away those who were about to question him left. Even the officer was alarmed. He realised that he had put Paul, a Roman citizen, in chains.

The commanding officer wanted to find out exactly what the Jews had against Paul. So the next day he let Paul out of prison. He ordered a meeting of the chief priests and all the members of the Sanhedrin. Then he brought Paul and had him stand in front of them.

Paul looked straight at the Sanhedrin. "My brothers," he said, "I have always done my duty to God. To this day I feel that I have done nothing wrong." Ananias the high priest heard this. So he ordered the men standing near Paul to hit him on the mouth. Then Paul said to him, "You pretender! God will hit you! You sit there and judge me by the law. But you yourself broke the law when you commanded them to hit me!"

Those who were standing near Paul spoke to him. They said, "How dare you talk like that to God's high priest!"

Paul replied, "Brothers, I didn't realise he was the high priest. It is written, 'Do not speak evil about the ruler of your people.'" *(from the Book of Exodus)*

Paul knew that some of them were Sadducees and the others were Pharisees. So he called out to the members of the Sanhedrin. "My brothers," he said, "I am a Pharisee. I come from a family of Pharisees. I believe that people will rise from the dead. That's why I am on trial." When he said this, the Pharisees and the Sadducees started to argue. They began to take sides. The Sadducees say that people will not rise from the dead. They don't believe there are angels or spirits either. But the Pharisees believe all these things.

People were causing trouble and making a lot of noise. Some of the teachers of the law who were Pharisees stood up. They argued strongly. "We find nothing wrong with this man," they said. "What if a spirit or an angel has spoken to him?" The people arguing were getting out of control. The commanding officer was afraid that Paul would be torn to pieces by them. So he ordered the soldiers to go down and take him away from them by force. The officer had told them to bring Paul into the fort.

The next night the Lord stood near Paul. He said, "Be

brave! You have told people about me in Jerusalem. You must do the same in Rome."

The next morning some Jews gathered secretly to make plans against Paul. They made a promise to themselves. They promised that they would not eat or drink anything until they killed him. More than 40 men took part in this plan. They went to the chief priests and the elders. They said, "We have made a special promise to God. We will not eat anything until we have killed Paul. Now then, you and the Sanhedrin must make an appeal to the commanding officer. Ask him to bring Paul to you. Pretend you want more facts about his case. We are ready to kill him before he gets here."

But Paul's nephew heard about this plan. So he went into the fort and told Paul.

Then Paul called one of the commanders. He said to him, "Take this young man to the commanding officer. He has something to tell him." So the commander took Paul's nephew to the officer.

The commander said, "Paul, the prisoner, sent for me. He asked me to bring this young man to you. The young man has something to tell you."

The commanding officer took the young man by the hand. He spoke to him in private. "What do you want to tell me?" the officer asked.

He said, "Some Jews have agreed to ask you to bring Paul to the Sanhedrin tomorrow. They will pretend they want more facts about him. Don't give in to them. More than 40 of them are waiting in hiding to attack him. They have promised that they will not eat or drink anything until they have killed him. They are ready now. All they need is for you to bring Paul to the Sanhedrin."

The commanding officer let the young man go. But he gave him a warning. "Don't tell anyone you have reported this to me," he said.

Then the commanding officer called for two of his commanders. He ordered them, "Gather a company of 200 soldiers, 70 horsemen and 200 men armed with spears. Get them ready to go to Caesarea at nine o'clock tonight. Provide horses for Paul so that he may be taken safely to Governor Felix."

Here is the letter the officer wrote.

I, Claudius Lysias, am writing this letter.

I am sending it to His Excellency, Governor Felix.

Greetings.

The Jews grabbed Paul. They were about to kill him. But I came with my soldiers and saved him. I had learned that he is a Roman citizen. I wanted to know why they were bringing charges against him. So I brought him to their Sanhedrin. I found out that the charge against him was based on questions about their law. But there was no charge against him worthy of death or prison. Then I was told about a plan against the man. So I sent him to you at once. I also ordered those bringing charges against him to present their case to you.

The soldiers followed their orders. During the night they took Paul with them. They brought him as far as Antipatris. The next day they let the horsemen go on with him. The soldiers returned to the fort. The horsemen arrived in Caesarea. They gave the letter to the governor. Then they handed Paul over to him. The governor read the letter. He asked Paul where he was from. He learned that Paul was from Cilicia. So he said, "I will hear your case when those bringing charges against you get here." Then he ordered that Paul be kept under guard in Herod's palace.

Five days later Ananias the high priest went down to Caesarea. Some elders and a lawyer named Tertullus went with him. They brought their charges against Paul to the governor. So Paul was called in. Tertullus began to bring the charges against Paul. He said to Felix, "We have enjoyed a long time of peace while you have been ruling. You are a wise leader. You have made this a better nation. Most excellent Felix, we gladly admit this everywhere and in every way. And we are very thankful. I don't want to bother you. But would you be kind enough to listen to us for a short time?

"We have found that Paul is a troublemaker. This man stirs up trouble among Jews all over the world. He is a leader of those who follow Jesus of Nazareth. He even tried to make our temple impure. So we arrested him. Question him yourself. Then you will learn the truth about all these charges we are bringing against him."

The other Jews said the same thing. They agreed that the charges were true.

The governor motioned for Paul to speak. Paul said, "I know that you have been a judge over this nation for quite a few years. So I am glad to explain my actions to you. About 12 days ago I went up to Jerusalem to worship. You can easily check on this. Those bringing charges against me did not find me arguing with anyone at the temple. I wasn't stirring up a crowd in the synagogues or anywhere else in the city. They can't prove to you any of the charges they are making against me. It is true that I worship the God of our people. I am a follower of the Way of Jesus. Those bringing charges against me call it a cult. I believe everything that is in keeping with the Law. I believe everything that is in keeping with what is written in the Prophets. I have the same hope in God that these men themselves have. I believe that both the godly and the ungodly will rise from the dead. So I always try not to do anything wrong in the eyes of God or in the eyes of people.

"I was away for several years. Then I came to Jerusalem to bring my people gifts for those who were poor. I also came to offer sacrifices. They found me doing this in the temple courtyard. I had already been made pure and 'clean' in the usual way. There was no crowd with me. I didn't stir up any trouble. But there

are some other Jews who should be here in front of you. They are from Asia Minor. They should bring charges if they have anything against me. Let the Jews who are here tell you what crime I am guilty of. After all, I was put on trial by the Sanhedrin. Perhaps they blame me for what I said when I was on trial. I shouted, 'I believe that people will rise from the dead. That is why I am on trial here today.'"

Felix knew all about the Way of Jesus. So he put off the trial for the time being. "Lysias the commanding officer will come," he said. "Then I will decide your case." He ordered the commander to keep Paul under guard. He told him to give Paul some freedom. He also told him to allow Paul's friends to take care of his needs.

Several days later Felix came with his wife Drusilla. She was a Jew. Felix sent for Paul and listened to him speak about faith in Christ Jesus. Paul talked about how to live a godly life. He talked about how people should control themselves. He also talked about the time when God will judge everyone. Then Felix became afraid. "That's enough for now!" he said. "You may leave. When I find the time, I will send for you." He was hoping that Paul would offer him some money to let him go. So he often sent for Paul and talked with him.

Two years passed. Porcius Festus took the place of Felix.

But Felix wanted to do the Jews a favour. So he left Paul in prison.

Three days after Festus arrived, he went up from Caesarea to Jerusalem. There the chief priests and the Jewish leaders came to Festus. They brought their charges against Paul. They tried very hard to get

Festus to have Paul taken to Jerusalem. They asked for this as a favour. They were planning to hide and attack Paul along the way. They wanted to kill him. Festus answered, "Paul is being held at Caesarea. Soon I'll be going there myself. Let some of your leaders come with me. If the man has done anything wrong, they can bring charges against him there."

Festus spent eight or ten days in Jerusalem with them. Then he went down to Caesarea. The next day he called the court together. He ordered Paul to be brought to him. When Paul arrived, the Jews who had come down from Jerusalem stood around him. They brought many strong charges against him. But they couldn't prove that these charges were true.

Then Paul spoke up for himself. He said, "I've done nothing wrong against the law of the Jews or against the temple. I've done nothing wrong against Caesar."

But Festus wanted to do the Jews a favour. So he said to Paul, "Are you willing to go up to Jerusalem? Are you willing to go on trial there? Are you willing to face these charges in my court?"

Paul answered, "I'm already standing in Caesar's court. This is where I should go on trial. I haven't done anything wrong to the Jews. You yourself know that very well. If I am guilty of anything worthy of death, I'm willing to die. But the charges brought against me by these Jews are not true. No-one has the right to hand me over to them. I make my appeal to Caesar!"

Festus talked it over with the members of his court.

Then he said, "You have made an appeal to Caesar. To Caesar you will go!"

A few days later King Agrippa and Bernice arrived in Caesarea. They came to pay a visit to Festus. They were spending many days there. So Festus talked with the king about Paul's case. He said, "There's a man here that Felix left as a prisoner. When I went to Jerusalem, the Jewish chief priests and the elders brought charges against the man. They wanted him to be found guilty.

"I told them that this is not the way Romans do things. We don't judge people before they have faced those bringing charges against them. They must have a chance to argue against the charges for themselves. When the Jewish leaders came back with me, I didn't waste any time. I called the court together the next day. I ordered the man to be brought in. Those bringing charges against him got up to speak. But they didn't charge him with any of the crimes I had expected. Instead, they argued with him about their own beliefs. They didn't agree about a man named Jesus. They said Jesus was dead, but Paul claimed Jesus was alive. I had no idea how to look into such matters. So I asked Paul if he would be willing to go to Jerusalem. There he could be tried on these charges. But Paul made an appeal to have the Emperor decide his case. So I ordered him to be held until I could send him to Caesar."

Then Agrippa said to Festus, "I would like to hear this man myself."

Festus replied, "Tomorrow you will hear him."

The next day Agrippa and Bernice arrived. They were treated like very important people. They entered the courtroom. The most important military officers and the leading men of the city came with them. When Festus gave the command, Paul was brought in. Festus said, "King Agrippa, and everyone else here, take a good look at this man! A large number of Jews have come to me about him. They came to me in Jerusalem and also here in Caesarea. They keep shouting that he shouldn't live any longer. I have found that he hasn't done anything worthy of death. But he made his appeal to the Emperor. So I decided to send him to Rome. I don't have anything certain to write about him to His Majesty. So I have brought him here today. Now all of you will be able to hear him. King Agrippa, it will also be very good for you to hear him. As a result of this hearing, I will have something to write. It doesn't make sense to send a prisoner on to Rome without listing the charges against him."

Agrippa said to Paul, "You may now present your case."

So Paul motioned with his hand. Then he began to present his case. "King Agrippa," he said, "I am happy to be able to stand here today. I will answer all the charges brought against me by the Jews. I am very pleased that you are familiar with Jewish ways. You know the kinds of things they argue about. So I beg you to be patient as you listen to me.

"The Jewish people all know how I have lived ever since I was a child. They know all about me from the beginning of my life. They know how I lived in my own country and in Jerusalem. They have known me for a long time. So if they wanted to, they could tell you how I have lived. I have lived by the rules of the Pharisees. Those rules are harder to obey than those of any other Jewish group. Today I am on trial because of the hope I have. I believe in what God promised our people of long ago. It is the promise that our 12 tribes are hoping to see come true. Because of this hope they serve God with faithful and honest hearts day and night. King Agrippa, it is also because of this hope that these Jews are bringing charges against me. Why should any of you think it is impossible for God to raise the dead?

"I believed that I should oppose the name of Jesus of Nazareth. So I did everything I could to oppose his name. That's just what I was doing in Jerusalem. On the authority of the chief priests, I put many of the Lord's people in prison. I agreed that they should die. I often went from one synagogue to another to have them punished. I tried to force them to speak evil things against Jesus. All I wanted to do was hurt them. I even went looking for them in the cities of other lands.

"On one of these journeys I was on my way to Damascus. I had the authority and commission of the chief priests. About noon, King Agrippa, I was on the road. I saw a light coming from heaven. It was brighter than the sun. It was shining around me and my companions. We all fell to the ground. I heard a voice speak to me in the Aramaic language. 'Saul! Saul!' it said. 'Why are you opposing me? It is hard for you to go against what you know is right.'

"Then I asked, 'Who are you, Lord?'

"'I am Jesus,' the Lord replied. 'I am the one you are opposing. Now get up. Stand on your feet. I have appeared to you to appoint you to serve me. And you must tell other people about me. You must tell others that you have seen me today. You must also tell them that I will show myself to you again. I will save you from your own people and from the Gentiles. I am sending you to them to open their eyes. I want you to turn them from darkness to light. I want you to turn them from Satan's power to God. I want their sins to be forgiven. They will be forgiven when they believe in me. They will have their place among God's people.'

"So then, King Agrippa, I obeyed the vision that appeared from heaven. First I preached to people in Damascus. Then I preached in Jerusalem and in all Judea. And then I preached to the Gentiles. I told them to turn away from their sins to God. The way they live must show that they have turned away from their sins. That's why some Jews grabbed me in the temple courtyard and tried to kill me. But God has helped me to this day. So I stand here and tell you what is true. I tell it to everyone, both small and great. I have been saying nothing different from what the prophets and Moses said would happen. They said the

Messiah would suffer. He would be the first to rise from the dead. He would bring the message of God's light. He would bring it to his own people and to the Gentiles."

While Paul was still presenting his case, Festus interrupted. "You are out of your mind, Paul!" he shouted. "Your great learning is driving you crazy!"

"I am not crazy, most excellent Festus," Paul replied. "What I am saying is true and reasonable. The king is familiar with these things. So I can speak openly to him. I am certain he knows everything that has been going on. After all, it was not done in secret. King Agrippa, do you believe the prophets? I know you do."

Then Agrippa spoke to Paul. "Are you trying to talk me into becoming a Christian?" he said. "Do you think you can do that in such a short time?"

Paul replied, "I don't care if it takes a short time or a long time. I pray to God for you and all who are listening to me today. I pray that you may become like me, except for these chains."

The king stood up. The governor and Bernice and those sitting with them stood up too. They left the room and began to talk with one another. "Why should this man die or be put in prison?" they said. "He has done nothing worthy of that!"

Agrippa said to Festus, "This man could have been set free. But he has made an appeal to Caesar."

It was decided that we would sail for Italy. Paul and some other prisoners were handed over to a Roman commander named Julius. He belonged to the Imperial Guard. We boarded a ship from Adramyttium. It was about to sail for ports along the coast of Asia Minor. We headed out to sea. Aristarchus was with us. He was a Macedonian from Thessalonica.

The next day we landed at Sidon. There Julius was kind to Paul. He let Paul visit his friends so they could give him what he needed. From there we headed out to sea again. We passed the calmer side of Cyprus because the winds were against us. We sailed across the open sea off the coast of Cilicia and Pamphylia. Then we landed at Myra in Lycia. There the commander found a ship from Alexandria sailing for Italy. He put us on board. We moved along slowly for many days. We had trouble getting to Cnidus. The wind did not let us stay on course. So we passed the calmer side of Crete, opposite Salmone. It was not easy to sail along the coast. Then we came to a place called Fair Havens. It was near the town of Lasea.

A lot of time had passed. Sailing had already become dangerous. By now it was after the Day of Atonement, a day of fasting. So Paul gave them a warning. "Men," he said,

"I can see that our trip is going to be dangerous. The ship and everything in it will be lost. Our own lives will be in danger also." But the commander didn't listen to what Paul said. Instead, he followed the advice of the pilot and the ship's owner. The harbour wasn't a good place for ships to stay during winter. So most of the people decided we should sail on. They hoped we would reach Phoenix. They wanted to spend the winter there. Phoenix was a harbour in Crete. It faced both southwest and northwest.

A gentle south wind began to blow. The ship's crew thought they saw their chance to leave safely. So they pulled up the anchor and sailed along the shore of Crete. Before very long, a wind blew down from the island. It had the force of a hurricane. It was called the Northeaster. The ship was caught by the storm. We could not keep it sailing into the wind. So we gave up and were driven along by the wind. We passed

the calmer side of a small island called Cauda. We almost lost the lifeboat that was tied to the side of the ship. So the men lifted the lifeboat on board. Then they tied ropes under the ship itself to hold it together. They were afraid it would get stuck on the sandbars of Syrtis. So they lowered the sea anchor and let the ship be driven along. We took a very bad beating from the storm. The next day the crew began to throw the ship's contents overboard. On the third day, they even threw the ship's tools and supplies overboard with their own hands. The sun and stars didn't appear for many days. The storm was terrible. So we gave up all hope of being saved.

The men had not eaten for a long time. Paul stood up in front of them. "Men," he said, "you should have taken my advice not to sail from Crete. Then you would have avoided this harm and loss. Now I beg you to be brave. Not one of you will die. Only the ship will be destroyed. I belong to God and serve him. Last night his angel stood beside me. The angel said, 'Do not be afraid, Paul. You must go on trial in front of Caesar. God has shown his grace by sparing the lives of all those sailing with you.' Men, continue to be brave. I have faith in God. It will happen just as he told me. But we must run the ship onto the beach of some island."

On the 14th night the wind was still pushing us across the Adriatic Sea. About midnight the sailors had a feeling that they were approaching land. They measured how deep the water was. They found that it was 120 feet deep. A short time later they measured the water again. This time it was 90 feet deep. They were afraid we would crash against the rocks. So they dropped four anchors from the back of the ship. They prayed that daylight would come. The sailors wanted to escape from the ship. So they let the lifeboat down into the sea. They pretended they were going to lower some anchors from the front of the ship. But Paul spoke to the commander and the soldiers. "These men must stay with the ship," he said. "If they don't, you can't be saved." So the soldiers cut the ropes that held the lifeboat. They let it drift away.

Just before dawn Paul tried to get them all to eat. "For the last 14 days," he said, "you have wondered what would happen. You have gone without food. You haven't eaten anything. Now I am asking you to eat some food. You need it to live. Not one of you will lose a single hair from your head." After Paul said this, he took some bread and gave thanks to God. He did this where they all could see him. Then he broke it and began to eat. All of them were filled with hope. So they ate some food. There were 276 of us on board. They ate as much as they wanted. They needed to make the ship lighter. So they threw the rest of the corn into the sea.

When daylight came, they saw a bay with a sandy beach. They didn't recognise the place. But they decided to run the ship onto the beach if they could. So they cut the anchors loose and left them in the sea.

At the same time, they untied the ropes that held the rudders. They lifted the sail at the front of the ship to the wind. Then they headed for the beach. But the ship hit a sandbar. So the front of it got stuck and wouldn't move. The back of the ship was broken to pieces by the pounding of the waves.

The soldiers planned to kill the prisoners. They wanted to keep them from swimming away and escaping. But the commander wanted to save Paul's life. So he kept the soldiers from carrying out their plan. He ordered those who could swim to jump overboard first and swim to land. The rest were supposed to get there on boards or other pieces of the ship. That is how everyone reached land safely.

When we were safe on shore, we found out that the island was called Malta. The people of the island were unusually kind. It was raining and cold. So they built a fire and welcomed all of us. Paul gathered some sticks

and put them on the fire. A poisonous snake was driven out by the heat. It fastened itself on Paul's hand. The people of the island saw the snake hanging from his hand. They said to one another, "This man must be a murderer. He escaped from the sea. But the female god Justice won't let him live." Paul shook the snake off into the fire. He was not harmed. The people expected him to swell up. They thought he would suddenly fall dead. They waited for a long time. But they didn't see anything unusual happen to him. So they changed their minds. They said he was a god.

Publius owned property nearby. He was the chief official on the island. He welcomed us to his home. For three days he took care of us. He treated us with kindness. His father was ill in bed. The man suffered from fever and dysentery. So Paul went in to see him. Paul prayed for him. He placed his hands on him and healed him. Then the rest of the ill people on the island came. They too were healed. The people of the island honoured us in many ways. When we were ready to sail, they gave us the supplies we needed.

After three months we headed out to sea. We sailed in a ship from Alexandria that had stayed at the island during the winter. On the front of the ship the figures of twin gods were carved. Their names were Castor and Pollux. We landed at Syracuse and stayed there for three days. From there we sailed to Rhegium. The next day the south wind came up. The day after that, we reached Puteoli. There we found some believers.

They invited us to spend a week with them. At last we came to Rome. The believers there had heard we were coming. They travelled as far as the Forum of Appius and the Three Taverns to meet us. When Paul saw these people, he thanked God for them and was encouraged by them. When we got to Rome, Paul was allowed to live by himself. But a soldier guarded him.

Three days later Paul called a meeting of the local Jewish leaders. When they came, Paul spoke to them. He said, "My brothers, I have done nothing against our people. I have also done nothing against what our people of long ago practised. But I was arrested in Jerusalem. I was handed over to the Romans. They questioned me. And they wanted to let me go. They saw I wasn't guilty of any crime worthy of death. But the Jews objected, so I had to make an appeal to Caesar. "I certainly did not mean to bring any charge against my own people. I share Israel's hope. That is why I am held with this chain. So I have asked to see you and talk with you."

They replied, "We have not received any letters from Judea about you. None of our people here from Judea has reported or said anything bad about you. But we want to hear what your ideas are. We know that people everywhere are talking against those who believe as you do."

They decided to meet Paul on a certain day. At that time even more people came to the place where he was staying. From morning until evening, he told them about God's kingdom. Using the Law of Moses and

the Prophets, he tried to get them to believe in Jesus. Some believed what he said, and others did not. They didn't agree with one another. They began to leave after Paul had made a final statement. He said, "The Holy Spirit was right when he spoke to your people long ago. Through Isaiah the prophet the Spirit said,

"'Go to your people. Say to them,
"You will hear but never understand.
    You will see but never know what you are
        seeing."
These people's hearts have become stubborn.
    They can barely hear with their ears.
    They have closed their eyes.
Otherwise they might see with their eyes.
    They might hear with their ears.
    They might understand with their hearts.
They might turn, and then I would heal them.'

(from the prophet Isaiah)

"Here is what I want you to know. God has sent his salvation to the Gentiles. And they will listen!"

For two whole years Paul stayed there in a house he rented. He welcomed all who came to see him. He preached boldly about God's kingdom. He taught people about the Lord Jesus Christ. And no-one could keep him from teaching and preaching about these things.

Living the story

God has always wanted every one of us to play a significant part in his story. He wanted the first people to care for his creation and help it thrive, but they chose to do things their own way. We see examples of selfish people hurting others every day.

Luke shared with Theo that King Jesus showed us a new way of living. We are to live with him as King and when we do this, we listen and do what he asks of us. He asks us to love and serve everyone, even people we really don't like because that is what he did. And he asks us to sacrifice ourselves and what we want in order to invite others to live in the kingdom of Jesus. This is how we are invited to be part of God's family as we see the ultimate sacrifice Jesus made for us. This story of King Jesus is part of a bigger story found throughout the Bible. We are invited to join in this story. How is that possible?

1. Read and understand the Bible for yourself

If we are not familiar with the story itself, there's no chance of living our parts well. We must read both deeply and widely in the Bible, letting it soak into our lives. Then we will be prepared to live the story well. The more we read the Bible, the better readers we will become. Then we will become skilled at understanding and living what we read.

2. Commit to follow Jesus

We've all taken part in the brokenness and wrongdoing that came into the story near the beginning. The victory of Jesus now offers us the opportunity to have our lives turned around. Our sins can be forgiven. We can become part of God's story of new creation.

Turn away from your wrongdoing. God has acted through the death and resurrection of King Jesus to deal with evil—in your life and in the life of the world. His death was a sacrifice, and his resurrection a new beginning. Acknowledge that Jesus is the rightful ruler of the world, and commit to follow him and join with God's people.

3. Live your part

As followers of Jesus we are called to live his story where we are. But we do not have an exact script. Our history has not yet been written. And we can't just repeat lines from earlier in the story. So what do we do?

We read the Bible to understand what God has already done, especially through King Jesus, and to know how we carry this story forward. *The Bible helps us answer the most important questions about everything we say and do: Is this an appropriate way to live out the story of Jesus today? Does it show that Jesus really is my King?* This is how we put the Scriptures into action. Life's choices can be messy, but God has given us his word and promised us his Spirit to guide us on the way. You are God's artwork, created to do good works. May your life be a gift of beauty back to him.

The Story: Luke–Acts

For adults who also want to read the same epic journey of Jesus and his first followers, there is a special edition of Luke–Acts for them too, called *The Story*.

Using the same simple formatting and familiar reading experience that has made *Dear Theo* so engaging, *The Story* brings Luke's incredible account of the man who turned his world upside down to a wider audience*.

Why not take up the challenge to read Luke and Acts with your family, friends or church community? Choose the edition(s) best suited to your context and begin the journey.

To find out more about how you can use *Dear Theo* and *The Story*, visit our website at www.biblicaeurope.com

The Story uses the full NIV text.

Community Bible Experience

If you have enjoyed reading *Dear Theo*, then we'd love to introduce you to the full Community Bible Experience. It's a fresh and engaging way to read the whole Bible. Like *Dear Theo*, we've set it out in a way that makes it easy for you to read and understand. There are four exciting volumes which will take you through the complete story of the Bible.

Covenant History – Discover the beginnings of God's people.

The Prophets – Listen to God's messengers tell about hope and truth.

The Writings – Learn from stories, poetry and songs.

New Testament – Read the story of Jesus, his church and his return.

What's exciting about Community Bible Experience is everyone one gets to join in the journey, from grown-ups down to pre-schoolers. The whole church can read and talk about God's story together.

To find out more about Community Bible Experience and how to get involved, visit our website at www.biblicaeurope.com/cbe

Partners

Dear Theo, is a bible engagement project developed by Biblica – The International Bible Society, in partnership with:

- Child Evangelism Fellowship Ireland
- Fields of Life East Africa
- Scripture Union Northern Ireland
- Scripture Union Scotland
- Scottish Bible Society

Together, we are passionate about making God's word available and accessible to all.

Notes & Doodles

Notes & Doodles

Notes & Doodles

Notes & Doodles

Notes & Doodles

Notes & Doodles